"The Yellow Wall-Paper"

by Charlotte Perkins Gilman

A DUAL-TEXT CRITICAL EDITION

"The Yellow Wall-Paper"

by Charlotte Perkins Gilman

A DUAL-TEXT CRITICAL EDITION

Edited by Shawn St. Jean

OHIO UNIVERSITY PRESS

Athens

Ohio University Press, Athens, Ohio 45701
www.ohio.edu/oupress
© 2006 by Ohio University Press

Printed in the United States of America
All rights reserved

Ohio University Press books are printed on acid-free paper ⊗ ™

14 13 12 11 10 09 08 07 06   5 4 3 2 1

Frontispiece: Portrait of Charlotte Perkins Gilman, 1884.
Photograph by Hurd (Providence, Rhode Island).
Courtesy of The Schlesinger Library, Radcliffe Institute,
Harvard University, Charlotte Perkins Gilman Papers.

MS text used by permission of The Schlesinger Library, Radcliffe Institute
for Advanced Study, Harvard University, Charlotte Perkins Gilman Papers.

Library of Congress Cataloging-in-Publication Data
Gilman, Charlotte Perkins, 1860–1935.
  "The yellow wall-paper" by Charlotte Perkins Gilman : a dual-text critical edition /
edited by Shawn St. Jean.
     p. cm.
  Includes bibliographical references and index.
  ISBN-13: 978-0-8214-1653-2 (cloth : alk. paper)
  ISBN-10: 0-8214-1653-7 (cloth : alk. paper)
  ISBN-13: 978-0-8214-1654-9 (pbk. : alk. paper)
  ISBN-10: 0-8214-1654-5 (pbk. : alk. paper)
   1. Mentally ill women—Fiction. 2. Married women—Fiction. 3. Sex role—Fiction.
4. Gilman, Charlotte Perkins, 1860–1935. Yellow wallpaper. 5. Feminist fiction, American
—History and criticism. 6. Feminism and literature—United States. 7. Mentally
ill women in literature. 8. Married women in literature. 9. Sex role in literature.
10. Psychological fiction. 11. Feminist fiction. I. St. Jean, Shawn, 1967– II. Title.
  PS1744.G57Y45 2006
  813'.4—dc22
                                    2005038051

For Karen

Contents

Illustrations

Introduction

Basic Textual Issues and Hamlet

As you hold this book in your hands, two questions may naturally occur to you: what is a dual-text edition, and what will it do for me? The answer to both these questions relies on a distinction between "work" and "text." F. W. Bateson once asked, "If the *Mona Lisa* is in the Louvre, where [is] *Hamlet*?"[1] emphasizing the difference and indicating some complications. Although da Vinci's famous image appears as thousands of texts throughout the world, some of them poor and some of them excellent reproductions of the original painting (if it did not, relatively few of us would know what it looks like), the work itself, the masterpiece executed by da Vinci, exists in only one place.

The same is not true for Shakespeare's play, even if we consider handwritten and print versions only and leave performances aside—films starring Richard Burton, Mel Gibson, and Kenneth Branagh, to name a few; stage productions from the Globe Theatre opening down to tonight's community theater show—and disqualify other "impure" manifestations, such as brief allusions in *What Dreams May Come*, or major structural inspiration, as in *Rosencrantz and Guildenstern Are Dead*, and partial representations in photographs, paintings, sculptures, poems, songs, and even graffiti. These are all, broadly considered, texts derivative of *Hamlet*. Where indeed, then, is the "true" *Hamlet*?

Hypothetically, even if a perfect manuscript written by Shakespeare as he intended to bequeath it as his public legacy did survive, that document would still be *a* text but not *the* work. Why not? Because literary / linguistic works belong not to pen and paper, but to the abstract realm of language that we all share. Just as a school or a church is made not only of brick and mortar and steel but of flesh and blood and spirit too, *Hamlet* exists in those of us involved with it. In some sense, this is true of the *Mona Lisa,* also; however, the sense in which it is *not* true can be quickly discovered by anyone willing to test the Louvre's security systems. *Hamlet,* on the other hand, can be copied, mocked, satirized, and plagiarized—but never truly stolen.

In short, *Hamlet* exists on paper only as texts, and each of these representations is or contains a *variant,* making each text a different version of the work.

What then is a *good* text, and how are we to know? If we search the bookstores for *Hamlet,* we find editions negotiating the competing claims of quarto and folio, promptbook and fouled papers, and edited by the likes of Nicolas Rowe, Alexander Pope, and Samuel Johnson, among many others. Some texts differ substantially; and yet, if we are not to be overwhelmed by all this diversity, we agree to buy the *text*books our professors assign, read them, discuss and hear lectures on them, and are examined on them, often quite closely—on the tacit assumption that the work is well represented by them.

Modern scholarly texts are produced according to specific notions of what is "good." In the 1960s and 1970s, the Modern Language Association (MLA) Center for Editions of American Authors, later reincarnated as the Center for Scholarly Editions, began approving texts for canonical works according to rigorous guidelines. Since then, the disciplines of textual criticism and scholarly editing have evolved into a pluralistic state, in which dominant ideological views of texts, works, the roles of editors, and so on—notably those of the venerable "Greg-Bowers school" and the more recent "social constructionism" promoted by scholars such as Jerome McGann and D. F. McKenzie—coexist in tension.[2] This schism resulted, for example, in the disappearance of the term "definitive text" from editorial discourse and its replacement with the more neutral term "authoritative text," almost always preceded by "an" to indicate the interpretational and therefore competing status of multiple texts of works.

A dual- or multiple-text edition, presenting parallel texts or "versions" of the same work, is desirable for several reasons: (1) the concept of a monolithic work, a fallacy, is best complicated by a graphic demonstration of how the interpretive process is significantly affected by variants; (2) competing theories of good texts can be served by one volume—rather than by the practice, often dictated by economics, of arguing implicitly or directly that the one text offered is more authoritative than others on the market; although this process has proven invaluable to the development of textual criticism in the past half-century, end-product consumers have occupied a position akin to a jury that hears only one side of a case; (3) users of the edition will be in a position to observe how works are constructed and reconstructed for reasons that have less to do with aesthetics than with more mundane financial, temporal, and technological concerns; and (4) electronic technology has advanced to the level at which it can begin to overcome economic limitations. Although a multitext, paperbound *Hamlet* might still be cost-prohibitive, computers, especially as they enable electronic distribution via CD, DVD, and the Internet, can already do justice to the idea of multitexts.

The vast popularity of "The Yellow Wall-Paper," coupled with its relative compactness, does provide a practical example of the philosophical advantages of multitexting. However, the method in this volume is not to relativistically suggest that each text is equally good for any occasion; rather, it is to present both sides of the argument, so that informed readers can determine the most suitable text(s) for their purposes.

Advanced Textual Issues and "The Yellow Wall-Paper"

The editorial debate for the past several years concerning Gilman's story can be summarized thus: its first printing, in the *New England Magazine* for January 1892, and the surviving fair-copy manuscript, contain the only texts with authority (that is, they substantially reflect the *author's* intentions). No other text derived second- or third-hand shows evidence of control in any detail by the author; thus only one of these two texts would be traditionally acceptable as the basis for a scholarly critical edition. I offer the following account, based on documentary, bibliographic, and biographical evidence, in support of this critical assumption.

Gilman sent a fair-copy manuscript of "The Yellow Wall-Paper" from Pasadena, California, to William Dean Howells in Boston on August 28, 1890. Howells passed the story on to Horace Scudder of the *Atlantic Monthly,* who returned the manuscript to Gilman, attaching a handwritten rejection card, which reads: "Dear Madam: W. Howells has handed me this story. I could not forgive myself if I made others as miserable as I have made myself! Sincerely Yours, H. E. Scudder."

Having received the rejected manuscript from Scudder, she sent it promptly "to Mr. Austin" on October 26. Henry Austin, whose name is attached to "Traveller Literary Syndicate" in Gilman's manuscript log,[3] had written to Gilman weeks before, apparently soliciting manuscripts as a literary agent.

Gilman's autobiography, published in 1935, records that Austin

> placed [the story] with the *New England Magazine.* Time passed, much time, and at length I wrote to the editor of that periodical to this effect:
>
> *Dear Sir,*
>
> *A story of mine, 'The Yellow Wallpaper,' was printed in your issue of May, 1891. Since you do not pay on receipt of ms. nor on publication, nor within six months of publication, may I ask if you pay at all, and if so at what rates?*

They replied with some heat that they had paid the agent, Mr Austin. He, being taxed with it, denied having got the money.[4]

There would be no reason to doubt Gilman's word if it were not that a slightly different account also descends to us.

Nearly three decades later, Howells reprinted "The Yellow Wall-Paper" in his 1920 collection *The Great Modern American Stories: An Anthology.* In "A Reminiscent Introduction," he recalls: "Horace Scudder (then of *The Atlantic*) said in refusing [the story] that it was so terribly good that it ought never to be printed. But terrible and too wholly dire as it was, I could not rest until I had corrupted the editor of *The New England Magazine* into publishing it."[5] Gilman's account of Austin's agency would appear to conflict with Howells's self-promotion here. But, as it turns out, Howells's and Gilman's accounts are not mutually exclusive, if we step back in order to sort out the relationships of several people.

On March 1, 1890, while Gilman was composing "The Yellow Wall-Paper," she submitted a poem, "Similar Cases," to the *Nationalist,* a periodical edited by one Henry Willard Austin. The poem was published just over a month later in the April *Nationalist.* Meanwhile, on March 11, Gilman sent her short story "The Giant Wistaria" to the *New England Magazine,* edited jointly by Edward Everett Hale and Edwin Doak Mead.

In early September 1890, "Similar Cases" was reprinted in the *New England Magazine.* This demand to reprint the poem was certainly a windfall for an unknown writer. Further entries in Gilman's records explain it. On September 16, Gilman sent another poem, "An Anti-Nationalist Wail," "to Uncle Edward Hale," and it was published in the December *New England Magazine.* Scattered entries in both Gilman's and her husband's diaries record that Edward Everett Hale married Emily Baldwin Perkins (the sister of Charlotte's father) in 1852 and that Charlotte was a frequent visitor as they usually wintered in Boston and summered in Matunuck, Rhode Island, until he died in 1909.[6] Gilman apparently meant to make the most of this relationship-through-marriage: on October 26, 1890, she sent "Mer-songs, etc. to E. E. Hale," otherwise known as "Uncle Edward ([of the] Traveller Literary Syndicate)." The "Mer-songs" were not accepted, but her short story "The Giant Wistaria" was, and appeared in the June 1891 issue of the *New England Magazine.* By then Hale had left the magazine, but he retained close ties with Mead, who remained. In short, the publication of "The Yellow Wall-Paper" in January 1892 made a total of two poems and two short stories placed in the magazine in a sixteen-month period during which Gilman's "Uncle Edward" was either coeditor or a friend of the editor there.

The linking of "Uncle Edward" to "Traveller Literary Syndicate" in the manuscript log provokes interest. The specific business name, about which nothing has been discovered, sounds much like one of the literary agencies that advertised their willingness to "undertake every kind of work required between author and publisher"; some of those advertisements are glued to the inside back cover of Gilman's logbook. According to her diary, on September 23, 1890, Gilman had received an invitation from "Mr. Henry Austin, 'Traveller Literary Syndicate'" to submit material; one is reminded that Henry Willard Austin published Gilman's first poem and that Hale reprinted it in short order. It seems reasonable to conclude that Henry Willard Austin and Henry Austin are the same person, and that Austin and Hale, and perhaps others, constituted an agency of the "one hand washes the other" ilk, from whose patronage Gilman benefited.

And what role did Howells really play? As Julie Bates Dock has pointed out, *New England Magazine* coeditor Edwin Doak Mead was Howells's younger cousin by marriage and had been brought to Boston by Howells as a teenager.[7] Howells's "Reminiscent Introduction" could be taken for a claim that *he* received Scudder's rejection and then exerted pressure on his cousin to print the story. Scudder likely spoke directly to Howells about the story's inappropriateness for the *Atlantic,* and Howells learned somehow (through Mead, Hale, Austin, or Gilman herself) that the story had gone on to Mead's office at the magazine. If Howells put in a word for the story, Gilman may not have known about it or felt it important enough to mention in her autobiography, given her publishing history and preexisting connections at the *New England Magazine.* Conversely, Howells may not have reckoned properly with Gilman's own connections and thus may have given himself more than his fair share of credit.

In my interpretation, these circumstances (from which I have omitted many details) are crucial to the textual situation of "The Yellow Wall-Paper." The work called "The Yellow Wall-Paper" as transmitted via manuscript text through the *New England Magazine* text seems to have gone beyond Gilman's control: the story was placed through an intermediary agent or agents who, enabled by personal ties, circumvented the usual submission procedures. These procedures would normally have included an author's continued textual control (most importantly, by correcting proofs for errors introduced or missed by the compositors setting type) after acceptance, but no proofs are mentioned in any source. Gilman lived at the time in California, three thousand miles away from the publisher, and was beholden to the agency of her husband and others when dealing with Boston's literary community.

Further, Gilman, never well-off financially, was not compensated for the work and received very little even when the story was published in book form by Small,

Maynard (1899) and later as a contribution to William Dean Howells's collection. For this reason, she never had any incentive to revise the magazine text, which introduced more than four hundred major and minor variants from the manuscript. With respect to authorial control, then, Gilman's experiences with the story certainly do not mirror those of better-known nineteenth- and twentieth-century authors such as Thackeray, Tennyson, and Eliot, who viewed successive printings as opportunities for revision and correction. However, she may be more representative of vast numbers of minor, less privileged writers whose relationships with publishers were more tenuous.

The first critical edition of the story to emphasize textual concerns was brought out in 1998 by Julie Bates Dock.[8] Dock's choice of the magazine printing as her copy-text rests on two essential assumptions, which are worth reconsidering here: the first is contingent on her theoretical orientation and the second on her treatment of evidence. First:

> The manuscript might disclose the author's personal inclinations for wording, spelling, or punctuation at the time it was inscribed, but it can shed no light on how it was received . . . after the combined efforts of editors, compositors, proofreaders, pressworkers, newsagents, and others had transmitted "The Yellow Wall-paper" to its first audience by way of the printed impression on the pages of *The New England Magazine*.[9]

Aligning herself with the social constructionism promoted in recent years by Jerome McGann and D. F. McKenzie, Dock relies on one of its basic tenets, that the creative process is self-consciously collaborative. As she put it in her *PMLA* article,

> Gilman's manuscript has no necessary textual priority, for she would have expected editors to regularize punctuation in accordance with standards of her day. Moreover, Gilman offered no objection to the minor variations from her manuscript, as far as we have been able to discover. In the absence of evidence that Gilman opposed printing-house changes, the first printing stands as the version that best embodies the story Gilman presented to her contemporaries.[10]

But when we consider that the story was probably accepted for publication and printed without Gilman's initial knowledge, without her being given the opportunity to correct proof, and without desperately needed remuneration, the notion that she "presented" the story to the public becomes highly relative. More importantly, her private expectations and what she might have consented to, preferred, or opposed are being spoken for by the editor of the critical edition without recourse to evidence of any kind; indeed, "the absence of evidence," or what has remained undiscovered, is cited to buttress the theoretical speculation that authors are often willfully careless as to the accidentals (punctuation, paragraphing, spelling, and so on) of their texts. Because selection of copy-text, which is the crucial basis of the critical edition, depends on and dictates the accidental texture of its text, the circular logic of Dock's position should be emphasized here: Authors do not care about spelling, punctuation, paragraphing, and so on—that is why publisher's agents take care of such matters for them. And, because they know they do not have to attend to such matters, authors are careless about them.

As odd as it seems, this model may, in fact, work for many authors. However, this does not mean it works for most, and certainly not for all. In Gilman's case, Dock does the responsible thing by citing outside comments by Gilman concerning accidentals in order to establish a pattern of behavior. As Dock knows, this is a somewhat lawyerly procedure, since none of these comments pertains directly to the case of "The Yellow Wall-Paper." In fact, I would describe the situation as one of a broken chain of evidence; that is, one crucial bit of information is missing, a document that would establish beyond a reasonable doubt whether Gilman endorsed, grudgingly accepted, or opposed the more than four hundred changes to her text made by the *New England Magazine*. Dock has not erred by attempting to substitute reasoning and judgment for missing evidence, as all editors (and lawyers) must do at some point in every case; but this line of reasoning is driven by a specific theoretical bias that must be acknowledged: that authors only *initiate* a highly collaborative process. Those favoring the manuscript text may, conversely, tend to see nonauthorial changes to a work only as corruption.

At least, this is how the arguments found in single-text critical editions run, and those debates will continue for some time to come; however, without dispensing with the vital work of arguing for "better" texts of works, multiple-text editions (most of which will probably be electronic editions because of the high costs involved in producing paper editions) open up new possibilities for doing justice to works. Following are some of the substantive variants (changes in wording) between the two authoritative texts of "The Yellow Wall-Paper" as presented in this edition, and brief suggestions of how they can affect interpretation:

It is very seldom that mere ordinary people like John and I secure ancestral halls for the summer. (MS, 1–2)[11]

It is very seldom that mere ordinary people like John and myself secure ancestral halls for the summer. (NEM, 1–2)[12]

Besides I don't want anybody to get that woman out at night but me. (MS, 403)

Besides, I don't want anybody to get that woman out at night but myself. (NEM, 429–30)

Although pronoun choice is often considered insignificant, occasionally it may be exploited to good effect or at least interpreted as if it had been. In 1989, Catherine Golden, apparently without knowledge of the alterations from manuscript, devoted considerable attention to the narrator's use of "I," "one," "he," and other pronouns: "In introducing 'myself' and 'John,' the narrator intensifies her awkward position in her sentence and society; she is not even on par with 'ordinary people like John.'"[13] In other words, "myself" is a more diminutive, less assertive choice than "I," as Henry David Thoreau insisted in *Walden*. Ironically, the *New England Magazine* text began with a large pictorial "I" (the first word of the story being "It," described by Golden in this edition) but in its linguistic text replaced "John and I" with "John and myself." Next,

I never saw so much expression in an inanimate thing before, and we all know how much expression ~~they~~ inanimate things have! (MS, 135–37)

I never saw so much expression in an inanimate thing before, and we all know how much expression they have! (NEM, 146–47)

Half the time now I am lazy, awfully lazy, and lie down ~~around~~ ever so much. (MS, 218)

Half the time now I am awfully lazy, and lie down ever so much. (NEM, 231)

The narrator frequently repeats herself, perhaps suggesting something about her psychological makeup: obsession, or at least fixation. The central image of the story, the wall-paper, is the "inanimate thing" deliberately double-referenced for effect (as shown by Gilman's crossing out of the pronoun "they") in the first example. Notice that the magazine overrode this cancellation, presumably to avoid unnecessary repetition, but respected Gilman's next cancellation, "around" for "down."

And dear John gathered me up in his [next word interlined] strong arms . . . (MS, 228)

And dear John gathered me up in his arms, . . . (NEM, 241)

He might even take me away. (MS, 345)

He might even want to take me away. (*NEM*, 362–63)

It would be a shame to break that beautiful strong door! (MS, 482)

It would be a shame to break down that beautiful door! (*NEM*, 518)

Before John's fainting spell (or death?) at the very end of the story, the manuscript narrator associates her husband with strength, both physical (i.e., his ability to carry her or break down strong doors) and mental (his scientific knowledge and domination of her). But the magazine's John is far less associated with strength in all of the above examples.

If I had not used it that blessed child would have! (MS, 235–36)

If we had not used it, that blessed child would have! (*NEM*, 249)

So of course I said no more on that score, and he went to sleep before long. (MS, 288)

So of course I said no more on that score, and we went to sleep before long. (*NEM*, 304)

The bedroom at the top of the mansion is sometimes occupied by both the narrator and her husband, and other times by her alone when John is away all night, as she believes, attending seriously ill patients. MS uses solitary pronouns that highlight the sense of isolation. More than one student of mine has suggested that John may be having extramarital affairs during his overnight absences; perhaps the magazine's agents wished to avoid emphasizing spousal neglect, or worse, infidelity.

It must be very unpleasant to be caught creeping by daylight! (MS, 398–99)

It must be very humiliating to be caught creeping by daylight! (*NEM*, 424–25)

Clearly, two different feelings are being contemplated here. The first connotes mere inconvenience at discovery, while the second expresses fear and a definitively embarrassing anticipation of discovery. To me, the manuscript reading jibes better with the story's conclusion: the narrator is "caught creeping" defiantly in the final scene, and may have been planning the confrontation with John for some time. If anything, she develops an air of pride in her creeping, and could hardly be humiliated by it.

Extratextual Issues and Summary of Essays

The market that dictates single-text critical editions based on arguments for certain texts of works has held sway for several decades. This means that even the kind of rudimentary observations I've made above, readings that could arise only by noting the *differences between texts,* have been precluded entirely or limited only to researchers, not because of aesthetic or theoretical undesirability, but simply on the basis of cost. However, the steadily rising material and production costs of even single-text print editions, accompanied by a general cultural movement toward electronic books, makes it likely that the scholarly and textbook publishers, who often operate on an even narrower profit margin than trade publishers because their print runs are smaller, will "go digital." Certain types of print books —art and photography, certainly—may continue to flourish, but fiction will probably be among the first migrants to widespread electronic form in the next decades. Books on tape and compact disc today; e-books and Internet subscriptions tomorrow.

With the removal of old financial obstacles that dictated the limited format of print editions, might we get more material from our critical editions? We already have print editions that offer, in addition to a critical text (and here I need look no further than editions of "The Yellow Wall-Paper"), an apparatus and tables of variants, historical and textual introductions, informational and bibliographic foot- and endnotes, contemporary reviews of the work, authors' correspondence, criticism, illustrations, timelines, legal documents, and related literary works (Dale M. Bauer's volume, for example, reprints a text of Kate Chopin's "The Story of an Hour"). Can variant texts, enabled by the convenience of electronic storage and access, be far behind?[14]

This volume on Charlotte Perkins Gilman's "The Yellow Wall-Paper" attempts to provide a limited model of the multiple-text edition in codex form—a sort of intermediate tool with which to test the benefits (and drawbacks) of multitexting. I have primarily assumed and argued, along with the contributors, that the two texts edited and presented here are both worth reading: Gilman's manuscript version as the result of an isolated, author-only compositional process; the *New England Magazine* version as an artifact reflecting the print and popular culture of 1890s America. A third text considered for inclusion, the Small, Maynard book printing of 1899, derives directly from the magazine and introduces only a few substantive variants; these are included in the variant list. The variant list has been designed for easy reading, and dispenses with the formal sigla (which even some scholars have complained of as "barbed-wire," or "code") of traditional critical editions.

The critical essays in the second section of this book were written exclusively for this volume, and aim to offer entirely new readings of the work enabled by awareness and appreciation of the differences between the two texts. The writers were asked to express a preferred text for the occasion, and at some point to demonstrate its origin. Catherine J. Golden reads the *New England Magazine* text specifically in the context of the "bibliographic codes" that defined the tale's first publication, most importantly the three illustrations executed by Jo H. Hatfield, which have not often been seen by students reading Gilman in anthologies. Denise D. Knight prefers the manuscript for its deeper ambivalence about the narrator's "insanity," a condition almost universally assumed by critics. Knight argues, rather, that a "deliberate act of rebellion" and rage may better explain the narrator's aberrant behavior, especially when juxtaposed with other women's works by Mary E. Wilkins Freeman and Kate Chopin. Allan H. Pasco also takes up the question of "female madness" in the context of unreliable narration, detailing a diagnosis of postpartum depression and related postpartum psychosis for the scribe of the manuscript text. He also indicates how the magazine text may have been revised by Gilman to enhance the authenticity of her account. Shawn St. Jean negotiates the variants between both versions in a deconstructive reading that proposes an authorial manuscript is less subject to "unraveling," or producing an unmanageable number of aporias, than a published text. This position grows out of the many possibilities for "Jane," a name whose referent has been debated by critics for three decades, and continues to be contested within the pages of this volume. As should be clear from these summaries, this edition as a whole cannot imply that either text is "better"—the essayists are evenly balanced between the two—but shows the overall benefit to the work and its readers when multiple perspectives are given voice.

Notes

1. Quoted in D. C. Greetham, *Textual Scholarship: An Introduction* (New York: Garland Publishing, 1992), 342.

2. Because this volume attempts to take a moderate position, drawing arguments from both the two "schools" of eclectic editing and social constructionist editing, I do not argue here for the fine points of what continues to develop as the fascinating discipline of textual criticism. A useful overview appears in Greetham. The seminal works in the field remain W. W. Greg, "The Rationale of Copy-Text," *Studies in Bibliography* 3 (1950): 19–36; Fredson Bowers, *Principles of Bibliographical Description* (New York: Russell and Russell, 1962); and Jerome McGann, *A Critique of Modern Textual Criticism* (Chicago: University of Chicago Press, 1983).

3. Excerpts from the unpaginated manuscript log are published in Julie Bates Dock's *"The Yellow Wall-paper" and the History of Its Publication and Reception* (University Park: Pennsylvania State University Press, 1998), 82–83. The complete original (*"Record of Mss.* Beginning *March 1st* 1890," box 37, vol. 23, Charlotte Perkins Gilman Papers, Schlesinger Library, Radcliffe College, Cambridge, Massachusetts) and Scudder's rejection card are available for study by scholars. My reconstructed timeline, which relies heavily on the manuscript log, clarifies the events described in the next several pages.

4. Charlotte Perkins Gilman, *The Living of Charlotte Perkins Gilman: An Autobiography* (New York: D. Appleton-Century, 1935), 119.

5. William Dean Howells, "A Reminiscent Introduction," in *The Great Modern American Stories: An Anthology* (New York: Boni and Liveright, 1920), vii–xiv.

6. See the *Dictionary of American Biography* (New York: Charles Scribner's Sons, 1932), 8:99–100, for general information on Hale; also Mary A. Hill, ed., *Endure: The Diaries of Charles Walter Stetson* (Philadelphia: Temple University Press, 1985), and Denise D. Knight, ed., *The Diaries of Charlotte Perkins Gilman,* 2 vols. (Charlottesville: University Press of Virginia, 1994), for Gilman's visiting practices, manuscript mailing and proofing habits, and personal and professional relationships.

7. Julie Bates Dock, Daphne Ryan Allen, Jennifer Palais, and Kristen Tracy, "'But One Expects That': Charlotte Perkins Gilman's 'The Yellow Wallpaper' and the Shifting Light of Scholarship," *PMLA* 111 (January 1996): 58.

8. After 1899 and until the 1970s, Gilman's story was published in several anthologies, most of them horror story collections, with no attention to textual accuracy. Even scholarly editions have not always identified their source texts correctly or have not always been edited perfectly: among these are Ann J. Lane's *The Charlotte Perkins Gilman Reader* (1980), Catherine Golden's *The Captive Imagination* (1992), and Thomas L. Erskine and Connie L. Richards's Rutgers University Press edition (1993). More recently, Carol Kivo's Harcourt Brace edition (1998) perpetuates the common error of identifying her source as the 1899 printing rather than the 1892 printing it actually derives from.

All but one of the scholarly editions available as of 2004 use the *New England Magazine* as a source text or what textualists call a "copy-text." The sole exception is Denise D. Knight's essential volume *"The Yellow Wall-Paper" and Selected Stories of Charlotte Perkins Gilman* (Newark : University of Delaware Press, 1994). Along with twenty-four previously published short stories, Knight chose to present for the first time a diplomatic transcription of the extant holograph manuscript housed in the Gilman Papers at Radcliffe College. In contrast to all previous editions of the story, in Knight's transcription "Gilman's spelling, punctuation, capitalization, indentations, and italics have been retained" with the objective "to preserve, rather than to correct or amend, Gilman's original text" (33).

Most famous and widely used of the editions that derive either directly or at second- or third-hand from the text of the *New England Magazine* is that produced by the Feminist Press. Its first edition of 1973, with Elaine R. Hedges's afterword, is widely credited with reintroducing the story to the scholarly community, though the myth repeated by so many critics and anthologists that the story went unprinted between William Dean Howells's edition of 1920 and the Feminist Press's "recovery" fifty-three years later has been disproved by the discovery of more than a dozen intervening editions (Dock, *History,* 4; Shawn St. Jean, "Gilman's Manuscript of 'The Yellow Wall-Paper': Toward a Critical Edition," *Studies in Bibliography* 51 [1998], 260n3). The first Feminist Press edition had several textual inaccuracies, including two dropped sentences, in addition to the inadvertent effacing of two section breaks by virtue of their placement at the bottoms of pages.

The second edition (1996) corrects these problems and includes a new "Note on the Text," which lists its "correction[s] of typographical errors" in *NEM*.

Dale Bauer's *Charlotte Perkins Gilman: The Yellow Wallpaper* (1998) is a rare volume in that it is explicitly directed at the classroom. The series to which it belongs, Bedford Cultural Editions, is described on the back cover as "a unique new literary reprint series of British and American titles in which the text of a work is accompanied by an abundance of thematically arranged historical and cultural documents. The documents—relevant excerpts from sources such as diaries, letters, periodicals, conduct books, legal documents, and literary works that parallel the themes of the main text—are carefully selected to give students a rich sense of a work's historical and cultural context." Series editors J. Paul Hunter and William E. Cain claim that "for each title, the volume editor has chosen the best teaching text of the main work and explained his or her choice," with the codicil that old spellings, punctuations, and usages have been preserved as worthy of historical study (vi).

The first published effort seriously to weigh the competing claims of all relevant texts (including Gilman's manuscript) of the story and to base its choices on both internal and external evidence is Julie Bates Dock's *"The Yellow Wall-paper" and the History of Its Publication and Reception* (1998). Billed as a "Critical Edition and Documentary Casebook," the volume includes the features scholars usually associate with meticulous textual work: a history of editions, a defense of its choice of copy-text, a word-division list, and a historical collation, in addition to diplomatic reproductions of many evidentiary documents and relevant correspondence and reviews.

9. Dock, *History*, 63. Dock believes, as do some scholars like Allan H. Pasco (in this volume) that *NEM* must have been set into type from a manuscript other than MS. See *History*, 46–50, for her statement of the case, which should be taken together with mine for the most complete account, as the reader decides for herself.

A brief example should indicate the complexity of the case. Dock cites several substantive variants between the texts "that do not suggest simple misreading of the manuscript by [*NEM*'s] compositors" (47) and therefore the editors must have "wielded a heavy hand at revision." Only "willful defiance of authorial instruction on the part of the compositor" (48) can explain some differences if MS were indeed the printer's copy. Gilman must have provided her publisher with another manuscript (MS2) from which to set type. MS2 has not been recovered.

I believe Dock's argument, compelling as an isolated theory, is less than cognizant of the day-to-day realities of the book trade. Anyone who has ever published so much as an article knows that seventy-five substantive alterations to a six-thousand-word piece of prose is not a "heavy" number; it is, in fact, routine. Given the conservative nature of the periodical and the controversial and even subversive nature of Gilman's story (recall that the *Atlantic Monthly* rejected it because it made the editor, Horace Scudder, "miserable"; William Dean Howells called it "terrible" both in private correspondence and in print), I am surprised there were not more extensive changes of purely editorial nature, as with the sentence dropped from *NEM*, "A sickly penetrating suggestive yellow." Some variants always occur by accident, others by editorial or even compositorial preference. The small number that remain may be difficult to solve more than a century later, but it hardly requires the invention of an intervening manuscript to account for them. Some are the result of purely typographical concerns. For example, the *New England Magazine* used a two-column type page with occasional illustrations and customarily began each piece of fiction with a large, stylized capital letter, necessitating a narrower column. The first variant from MS, "John and myself" (the complete fourth line of *NEM*) for "John and I," is less correct grammatically and might not have been substituted had it not supplied an appropriate number of characters for the line. "John and I" would have required an unattractive amount of spacing, "John and I secure" would have been too tight, and "John and I se-" would have been less desirable typographically than the solution that was adopted (see fig. 2 in this volume). The story's final variant, one Dock cites as primary evidence for a second manuscript, in which the MS reading "I had to creep over him!" was changed to "I had to creep over him every time!" in *NEM,* clearly furnished the extra line needed to make the two type columns end flush (see fig. 4 in this volume). That this evenness is not merely coincidental but rather an intended typographical feature is suggested by the nearly universal occurrence of the phenomenon throughout 1891 and 1892 numbers of the magazine, where only two of the almost three hundred articles end with uneven columns, as discovered by Elizabeth Lynch, editorial assistant for my *Studies in Bibliography* article. The interpretive consequences of the free rein likely taken by *NEM*'s agents in these cases are significant: both sentences are in key narrative positions that readers typically scrutinize, but that does not make them invulnerable to editorial interference when circumstances warrant.

10. Dock, "Shifting," 55.

11. Gilman, "The Yellow Wall-Paper" (manuscript), Charlotte Perkins Gilman Papers, Schlesinger Library, Radcliffe College, Cambridge, Massachusetts, line 1. Parenthetical references to Gilman's manuscript (MS) and the *New England Magazine* (NEM) refer to line numbers of the critical texts printed in this edition.

12. Gilman, "The Yellow Wall-Paper," *New England Magazine* 5 (January 1892), line 1 in this edition.

13. Catherine Golden, "The Writing of 'The Yellow Wallpaper': A Double Palimpsest," *Studies in American Fiction* 17 (Autumn 1989), 195. This remarkably close reading makes a strong case for the importance of "minor" substantive variants to interpretation, and implicitly, for retaining authorial usages *whenever* possible.

14. We have already seen a burgeoning precedent from a closely related genre: film. Hollywood "works" are now beginning to be produced without film, entirely by digital means. The rise in popularity (directly connected, notice, to plummeting costs) of movies on Digital Versatile Disc (DVD) is changing the way we consume film. On the economic end, videotape/disc rights that were once invoked years after original release for small profit are these days an integral part of producers' funding to make films in the first place. On the aesthetic end, videotape literally dictated a linear viewing experience, and background material was rare. Now, however, our private consumption of a film is not only enhanced by vast improvements in sound and picture quality, but often accompanied, in instantly accessible, nonlinear fashion, by theatrical trailers, making-of and historical documentaries, deleted scenes, alternate endings, director/producer/actor commentary superimposed on the soundtrack, production notes, biographies, storyboards and other artwork such as costume designs, and significantly, alternate versions. These currently are rare, but mainstream films like *Independence Day, Alien,* and *Manhunter* have been marketed in multiple-text "editions," versus films like *Blade Runner* that exist in profoundly different versions and media but still must be scrounged together for comparison by collectors.

The analogy is clear: DVD, once a tentative standard adopted only by serious film buffs, has gained widespread acceptance and actually raised the expectations of mass marketing of film. As I write, consumer-level "DVD-burner" drives for PCs have plummeted in price at an astounding rate. I would predict that these technological advances will help spur a rise in independent filmmaking and distribution in the not-too-distant future. And what of books, soon to be supplanted by "electronic editions," if the film industry is any indication?

1. Dual Texts

Timeline

Original source documents are located in the Charlotte Perkins Gilman Papers, Schlesinger Library, Radcliffe College.

Date	"The Yellow Wall-Paper"	Related Events	Source
1890			
Mar. 1		"Similar Cases" sent to Nationalist, ed. Henry Willard Austin	MS log
Mar. 11		"The Giant Wistaria" to *NEM*, ed. E. E. Hale and E. D. Mead, "via Walter" [Stetson]	MS log
Apr.		"Similar Cases" pub. in *Nationalist*	
June	sent to and rejected by *Scribners*[?]		MS log
Aug. 24	"finish copy of 'Yellow Wallpaper'"		diary
Aug. 28	sent to W. D. Howells		diary / MS log
Sept.		"Similar Cases" rpt. in *NEM*	
Sept. 16		sent "An Anti-Nationalist Wail" "to Uncle Edward Hale"	MS log
Sept. 23		receives letter from "Mr. Henry Austin, 'Traveller Literary Syndicate'" soliciting manuscripts	diary
Sept. 27		"all this week's mss. to Mr. Austin"	diary / MS log

Oct. 18	MS returned from Horace Scudder of *Atlantic:* "W. Howells has handed me this story"		card/ autobiography
Oct. 26	MS "to Mr. Austin"	"Mer-songs, etc. to E.E. Hale"/ "to Uncle Edward (Traveller Literary Syndicate)"	diary/MS log
Dec.		"An Anti-Nationalist Wail" pub. in *NEM*	
1891			
Feb. 14		receives copy of his *Vagabond Verses* from Henry Willard Austin	diary
June		"The Giant Wistaria" pub. in *NEM*	
Aug. 18		receives check for $14.00 from *NEM*	diary
1892			
Jan.	"The Yellow Wall-Paper" pub. in *NEM*		

Genealogy of Substantive Variants in Early Texts of "The Yellow Wall-Paper"

MS=fair-copy manuscript, ca. 1890–91
NEM=New England Magazine, January 1892
SM=Small, Maynard, & Co. book, mid- to late 1899

SUBSTANTIVE VARIANTS (differences between texts at or beyond the full word level) often enjoy a privileged status among single-text editors and interpreters, for several reasons: they are easier to detect; they usually occur less frequently than other types of variants, and so seem more significant; and they appear to be the product of *conscious intention* on someone's part—whether author, original editor, or compositor—to improve the work (this is often unture, as full words, phrases, and whole lines are routinely altered unintentionally). Finally, especially among nonadherents of the "Greg-Bowers" school of scholarly editing, copy-texts are often chosen for the perceived equality of their "substantive texture"; that is, how "good," how "literary," or even how long they are. This usually means that later texts are preferred as "most improved," both by the author in isolation and by the author in collaboration with publishers.

Contrarily, the rigorous following of the eclectic editing methods favored by the Greg-Bowers rationale proves difficult: selection of copy-text is made specifically to preserve the author's unique nonsubstantive ("accidental") usages, because substantives can be emended into the single copy-text from other texts with relative ease, while far more numerous accidentals cannot. This method is meant to produce a hybrid, "ideal" text, one fully reflecting the author's intentions, with both the "best" substantive and accidental texture.

These thorny questions of intentionality and what is best are circumvented by a multiple-text edition, which, while making the case for both sides, finally leaves the choice to the reader's, not the editor's, judgment.

The list is unemended, reflecting all original errors in the texts.

I. Substantive Variants Originating with NEM

(* indicates MS readings restored or further altered in SM.)

MS	Line	NEM	Line	SM
John and I	1	John and myself	1	John and myself
meet heavy	27	meet with heavy	30	meet with heavy
feel badly	30	feel bad	33	feel bad
and write about	31	and talk about	34	and talk about
road, and quite	33	road, quite	36	road, quite
anyhow, it has	42	anyhow, the place has	44	anyhow, the place has
for years and years	42	for years	44	for years
moonlit evening	44	moonlight evening	47	moonlight evening
windows, and	51	window, and	54	window, and
loving, hardly	55	loving, and hardly	58	loving, and hardly
takes every care	56	takes all care from me	60–61	takes all care from me
and I	56–57	and so I	61	and so I
sunlight galore	63	sunshine galore	67	sunshine galore
slow-turning sun	76	slow-turning sunlight	80	slow-turning sunlight
only nervous	91	only nervousness	96	only nervousness
is just to do	94	is to do	100	is to do
John was never	98	John never was	104	John never was
<u>is</u> as airy	109	is an airy	118	*is as airy
comfortable a room	110	comfortable room	118	*comfortable a room
bushes, the gnarly	114	bushes and gnarly	122	bushes and gnarly
wharf that belongs	115	wharf belonging	123–24	wharf belonging
pressure of ideas	123	press of ideas	131	press of ideas
two breadths	134	two breaths	144	*two breadths
inanimate things have	137	they have	147	they have
for I never	145	I never	156	I never
perfect—, an enthusiastic	154	perfect and enthusiastic	166	*perfect, an enthusiastic
when the sun	163	where the sun	175	where the sun
were worth	176	was worth	189	was worth
It is as good	188	It it as good	201	*It is as good
hasn't been	189	has nos been	202–3	*has not been
principles of design	192	principle of design	205	*principles of design
for a border	204	for a frieze	217	for a frieze
directly on it	207	directly upon it	220	directly upon it

MS	Line	NEM	Line	SM
grotesques	208	grotesque	221	*grotesques
lazy, awfully lazy	218	awfully lazy	231	awfully lazy
his strong arms	228	his arms	241	his arms
If I had	235	If we had	249	If we had
all round	252	all around	266	all around
it made me creepy	256	I felt creepy	270	I felt creepy
and our	284	and for our	299	and for our
he went to sleep	288	we went to sleep	304	we went to sleep
wasn't. I lay	289	wasn't, and lay	305	*wasn't,—I lay
whether the front	290	whether that front	306	whether that front
In a pattern	293	On a pattern	309	ON a pattern
a certain lack	293	a lack	309	a lack
following it it turns	298	following, it turns	313–14	following, it turns
tramples on you	299	tramples upon you	315	tramples upon you
behind is	312	behind it is	329	behind it is
behind, the dim	313	behind, that dim	330	behind,—that dim
something to	339–40	something more to	356–57	something more to
am much more quiet	340–41	am more quiet	357–58	am more quiet
even take	345	even want to take	362	even want to take
that paper	353	that wall-paper	372	that wall paper
A sickly penetrating suggestive yellow.	353–54	[sentence missing]	372	[sentence missing]
another thing	356	something else	375	something else
It creep	359	It creeps	379	It creeps
runs all round	371	runs round	396	*runs around
in very	383	and in the very	407	and in the very
unpleasant	399	humiliating	424	humiliating
but me	403	but myself	430	but myself
one at a time	405	one at one time	432	one at one time
try tearing it	411	try it	438	try it
John had to stay	424	John to stay	453	*John is to stay
till	425	until	454	until
servants, and the things	446	servants are gone, and the things are gone	476	servants are gone, and the things are gone
until	453	till	485	till
The bed	457	This bed	491	This bed
lift or push	458	lift and push	492	lift and push

MS	Line	NEM	Line	SM
till	458	until	492	until
do it of course!	465	do it. Of course not.	499	do it. Of course not.
all came out	469	all come out	503	all come out
break that beautiful strong door	482	break down that beautiful door	518	break down that beautiful door
front steps	487	front door	523	front door
slowly. ¶ I said	488	slowly, and said	524	slowly, and said
over him!	497–98	over him every time!	532	over him every time!

★ ★ ★ ★

II. Substantive Variants from NEM Originating in SM

(Does not include MS readings altered in NEM but restored or further altered in SM. These are part of the list above, marked by ★.)

MS	Line	NEM	Line	SM
playroom	63	playroom	67	playground
I get positively	132	I get positively	142	I got positively
skulk	164	skulk	176	sulk
how I wish	222–23	how I wish	235–36	how I wished
till it tired	229	till it tired	242	till he tired
any silly	232	any silly	246	my silly

Genealogy of Accidental Variants in Early Texts of "The Yellow Wall-Paper"

MS=fair-copy manuscript, ca. 1890
NEM=New England Magazine, January 1892

ACCIDENTAL VARIANTS (spelling, punctuation, paragraphing; changes at less than the full word level) are usually far more numerous than *substantive variants,* and—cumulatively, at least—can have as profound an effect on meaning. As W. W. Greg emphasized a half-century ago, the crucial point to recognize is that a copy-text, once chosen, is edited mostly with an eye toward substantives (both because they are far fewer and more manageable, and because they are seen as having more significance). This means that the accidental texture of the copy-text will often remain substantially unchanged in even a scholarly critical edition: thus, in considering which single-text edition to work from, the student would traditionally need to decide whether to interpret a text with an author's (sometimes careless and haphazard) accidentals (as in the case of MS), or a text incorporating the "regularization and correction" (also sometimes arbitrary and inconsistent) of publishing agents (*NEM* here). To put it another way, if an author's manuscript is available and the editor, for whatever reason, chooses to edit from a published version instead, the edition, for better or worse, will not reflect hundreds or even thousands of minor authorial usages.

Most critical editions do not offer a list of accidental variants, which is not really practicable for works longer than a short story. The list provided here emphasizes the deep and essential (but often overlooked) cumulative differences between the two texts in this edition, and thus between any two texts of any work. Because Gilman is almost universally believed not to have had any hand in SM (Small, Maynard, 1899), a list of its accidental variants has not been included.

The list is unemended, reflecting all original errors in the texts.

A Note on Paragraphing

The reader will notice that *NEM* is some thirty-five lines longer than MS in the present edition. This does not indicate a substantial addition of material, but is due to the insertion of paragraph breaks (marked as ¶ in the list of accidental variants that follows) by publisher's agents, resulting in a more fragmented narrative. However, Julie Bates Dock has rightly noted that the handwritten manuscript's paragraphing is open to interpretation; that being the case, I have elected to follow my own careful scrutiny of Gilman's handwriting practices and story-sense, rather than accept wholesale the judgment of *NEM*'s compositors, who worked under pressure, and often inconsistently, in conditions where time equaled money.

Occasionally multiple variants, when occurring in very close proximity, will appear in the same entry below. When more than one line is listed (e.g., 7–8), the reference invariably indicates a paragraph break in one text that does not exist in the other; a cursory scan of the right column reveals that *NEM* rebroke many of Gilman's paragraphs, while fusing some others.

By contrast, single-line-number references in the list refer to the lines in MS and *NEM* on which the variants actually occur, not necessarily to the line on which the phrase begins.

MS	Line/s	NEM	Line/s
<u>something</u> queer	5	something queer	5
about it. Else	5	about it. ¶ Else	5–6
in the extreme. ¶ He has no	8–9	in the extreme. He has no	9
perhaps,—I wouldn't say	11	*perhaps*—(I would not say	12
to my mind,—	12	to my mind—)	13
sick! And what	14	sick! ¶ And what	15–16
one do? If a	14	one do? ¶ If a	16–17
one to do? My brother	17	one to do? ¶ My brother	19–20
a good deal,—	26	a good deal—	29
place! ¶ It is quite	32–33	place! It is quite	35
hedges, and walls, and	35	hedges and walls and	37
garden. I never saw	37	garden! I never saw	39
such a garden, large	37	such a garden—large	39
greenhouses too,	40	greenhouses, too,	42
there <u>is</u> something	43	there is something	45
feel it. I even	44	feel it. ¶ I even	46–47
feel so I shall	48	feel so, I shall	51

MS	Line/s	NEM	Line/s
before him at least	49	before him, at least	52
downstairs, that	50	downstairs that	53
hangings; but	52	hangings! but	55
John wouldn't	52	John would not	55
direction; I have	55	direction. ¶ I have	59–60
the day, he takes	56	the day; he takes	60
value it more. He said	57	value it more. ¶ He said	61–62
perfect rest, and all	58	perfect rest and all	62
strength my dear" said he	59	strength, my dear," said he	63
big airy room	62	big, airy room	66
first, and then	63	first and then	67
should judge, for	64	should judge; for	68
little children and	64	little children, and	68
in the walls. The paint	65	in the walls. ¶ The paint	69–70
great patches, all around	66	great patches all around	71
my bed about	67	my bed, about	71
the room, low	68	the room low	72
low down. ¶ I never	68–69	low down. I never	72
my life. One of	69	my life. ¶ One of	73–74
patterns, committing	70	patterns committing	74
artistic sin. It is	70	artistic sin. ¶ It is	74–75
sun. It is a dull	76	sunlight. ¶ It is a dull	80–81
writing before since	83	writing before, since	87
cases are serious. I am glad	87	cases are serious. ¶ I am glad	91–92
not serious.	88	not serious!	92
John doesn't	90	John does not	94
any way. I meant	92	any way! ¶ I meant	97–98
burden already! Nobody	93	burden already! ¶ Nobody	99–100
able. To dress	94	able,—to dress	100
order things. It is	95	order things. ¶ It is	101–2
yet I can <u>not</u> be	97	yet I *cannot* be	103
wallpaper! At first	99	wall-paper! ¶ At first	105–6
meant to re-paper	99	meant to repaper	106
fancies. He said	101	fancies. ¶ He said	108–9
the wallpaper was changed	101	the wall-paper was changed	109
so on. "You know	103	so on. ¶ "You know	111–12
you good" he said	104	you good," he said	112

MS	Line/s	NEM	Line/s
three months rental.	105	three months' rental."	113
down stairs" I said	106	downstairs," I said	114
rooms there!"	106	rooms there."	114
down cellar if I	108	down cellar, if I	116
into the bargain!	108	into the bargain.	116
windows and things. It _is_	109	windows and things. ¶ It is	117–18
and of course I	110	and, of course, I	118
I wouldn't be	110	I would not be	119
oldfashioned flowers and bushes, the	114	old-fashioned flowers, and bushes and	122
trees. Out of	114	trees. ¶ Out of	122–23
story making	119	story-making	127
I try. It is so	124	I try. ¶ It is so	132–33
really well John	125	really well, John	134
in my pillowcase	127	in my pillow-case	135
about now. I wish	128	about now. ¶ I wish	136–37
faster. But I	128	faster. ¶ But I	137–38
broken neck, and	130	broken neck and	140
of it, and the	132	of it and the	142
those absurd unblinking	133	those absurd, unblinking	143
than the other. I never	135	than the other. ¶ I never	145–46
as a child, and	137	as a child and	147
toystore. I remember	139	toy-store. ¶ I remember	149–50
big old bureau	139	big, old bureau	150
friend. I used	141	friend. ¶ I used	151–52
things out—and no	145	things out, and no	156
hatred. Then the floor	148	hatred. ¶ Then the floor	159–60
wars. But I don't	151	wars. ¶ "But I don't	162–63
John's sister—such a dear	152	John's sister. Such a dear	164
I mustn't let her	153	I must not let her	165
perfect—,an enthusiastic—,	154	perfect and enthusiastic	166
lovely country too	159	lovely country, too	171
clearly then. But in the	162	clearly then. ¶ But in the	174–75
isn't faded, and	163	isn't faded and	175
just so,—I can	163	just so—I can	175
strange provoking formless	163	strange, provoking, formless	176
Mother and Nellie	170	mother and Nellie	181
do a _thing_—Jennie	171	do a thing. Jennie	183

MS	Line/s	NEM	Line/s
everything now. But	171	everything now. ¶ But	183–84
all the same. John says	172	all the same. ¶ John says	184–85
in the Fall.	173	in the fall.	185
my brother only more	175	my brother, only more	187
Besides it is such	176	Besides, it is such	188
so far. I don't	176	so far. ¶ I don't	188–89
querulous. I cry	178	querulous. ¶ I cry	190–91
at nothing and cry	178	at nothing, and cry	191
time. Of course	178	time. ¶ Of course	191–92
her to. So I walk	181	her to. ¶ So I walk	194–95
wall-paper. ¶ Perhaps	184–85	wallpaper. Perhaps	197
wall-paper! It dwells	185	wallpaper. ¶ It dwells	198–99
mind so! I lie	185	mind so! ¶ I lie	199–200
bed (—it's nailed	186	bed—it is nailed	200
I believe!) and	186	I believe—and	200
touched; and I	189	touched, and I	203
I determine, for	189	I determine for	203
thousandth time, that	190	thousandth time that	203
heard of. It is	194	heard of. ¶ It is	207–8
repeated of course	194	repeated, of course	208
debased Romanesque	197	"debased Romanesque"	210
But on the other hand they	199	But, on the other hand, they	212
direction. They have	203	direction. ¶ They have	216–17
the cross-lights fade	207	the crosslights fade	220
after all; the interminable	208	after all,—the interminable	221
a common center	208	a common centre	222
such a relief.	216	such a relief!	229
so much. John says	218	so much. ¶ John says	231–32
codliver-oil	219	cod liver oil	232
Julia. But he said	223	Julia. ¶ But he said	236–37
think straight—just this	226	think straight. Just this	239
weakness, I suppose	227	weakness I suppose	240
carried me up stairs	228	carried me upstairs	241
comfort, and all	230	comfort and all	243
keep well. He says	231	keep well. ¶ He says	244–45
There's <u>one</u> comfort	234	There's one comfort	247
horrid wall-paper. If	235	horrid wallpaper. ¶ If	248–49

MS	Line/s	NEM	Line/s
used it that blessed	235	used it, that blessed	249
would have! ¶ What	236–37	would have! What	249
escape! ¶ Why, I	237–38	escape! Why, I	250
after all. ¶ I can	240–41	after all, I can	252
a baby you see! Of	241	a baby, you see. ¶ Of	253–54
too wise, but I	242	too wise,—but I	254
same. There are	242	same. ¶ There are	255–56
ever will. Behind	243	ever will. ¶ Behind	256–57
every day. It is	244	every day. ¶ It is	257–58
numerous. And it's	245	numerous. ¶ And it is	258–59
stooping down, and	245	stooping down and	259
to think—¶ I wish	246–47	to think—I wish	260
is it little girl?	261	is it, little girl?	275
"Why, darling," said he	265	"Why, darling!" said he	279
leave before. The repairs	266	leave before. ¶ "The repairs	280–81
I can't possibly	266	I cannot possibly	281
you are away."	273	you are away!"	288
said he, with a big	274	said he with a big	289
Really, dear, you are	279	Really dear you are	294
in <u>body</u>, perhaps"—	281	in body, perhaps—"	296
stopped short; for he	281	stopped short, for he	296
stern reproachful look	282	stern, reproachful look	297
let <u>that</u> idea	285	let that idea	300
your mind. There	285	your mind! There	301
before long. ¶ He thought	288–89	before long. He thought	304
first, but I wasn't. I lay	289	first, but I wasn't, and lay	305
defiance of law that	294	defiance of law, that	310
there you are!	298	there you are.	314
down and tramples on	299	down, and tramples upon	315
That is, <u>sometimes</u>!	303	That is, sometimes!	319
long straight ray	307	long, straight ray	323
believe it. That is	308	believe it. ¶ That is	323–24
always. By moonlight	308	always. ¶ By moonlight	324–25
paper. At night, in any	309	paper. ¶ At night in any	326–27
by moonlight—it becomes <u>bars</u>!	311	by moonlight, it becomes bars!	328
pattern, I mean. And	311	pattern I mean, and	328
subdued,—quiet.	315	subdued, quiet.	332

MS	Line/s	NEM	Line/s
meal. It is	318	meal. ¶ It is	336–37
I don't sleep!	319	I don't sleep.	337
don't tell them	320	don't tell them	338
of John. He seems	321	of John. ¶ He seems	339–40
queer sometimes. And	322	queer sometimes, and	340
when he didn't know	325	when he did not know	343
I was looking—and	325	I was looking, and	343
And Jennie, too. ¶ I caught	327–28	And Jennie too. I caught	345
with the paper? she	331	with the paper—she	348
caught stealing and	331	caught stealing, and	348
But I know	336	But I know	353
than I was. John is	341	than I was. ¶ John is	358–59
me improve. ¶ He laughed	341–42	me improve! He laughed	359
other day and said	342	other day, and said	359
wall paper. I turned	343	wall-paper. ¶ I turned	360–61
of the wall-paper! ¶ He	344–45	of the wall-paper—he	362
away. I don't	345	away. ¶ I don't	363–64
developements	350	developments	368
daytime. In the	350	daytime. ¶ In the	368–69
perplexing. There are	351	perplexing. ¶ There are	369–70
I can not keep	352	I cannot keep	371
conscientiously. It is	353	conscientiously. ¶ It is	371–72
strangest yellow—that	353	strangest yellow, that	372
old foul bad yellow	355	old foul, bad yellow	373
smell! ¶ I noticed	356–57	smell! I noticed	375
or not the smell	359	or not, the smell	378
is here. It creeps	359	is here. ¶ It creeps	378–79
the house. I find	359	the house. ¶ I find	379–80
dining room	360	dining-room	380
the stairs. It gets	361	the stairs. ¶ It gets	381–82
my hair. Even when	361	my hair. ¶ Even when	382–83
it there is that smell!	362	it—there is that smell!	383
odor too!	363	odor, too!	385
smelled like. It is	364	smelled like. ¶ It is	386–87
is awful. I wake	366	is awful, I wake	389
over me. It used	367	over me. ¶ It used	390–91
the house to reach	367	the house—to reach	391

MS	Line/s	NEM	Line/s
the smell. But now	368	the smell. ¶ But now	392–93
mop-board	370	mopboard	395
round the room. ¶ It goes	371–72	round the room. It goes	396
furniture except the bed;	372	furniture, except the bed,	396
long straight even smooch	372	long, straight, even *smooch*	397
was done, and who	374	was done and who	398
did it for!	374	did it for.	398
at last. Through	377	at last. ¶ Through	401–2
no wonder! ¶ The woman	379–80	no wonder! The woman	404
shakes it! Sometimes	380	shakes it! ¶ Sometimes	404–5
only one and she	381	only one, and she	406
around fast. And her	381	around fast, and her	406
climb through. ¶ But	385–86	climb through. But	409
pattern, it strangles so. I	386	pattern—it strangles so; I	410
many heads. They get	387	many heads. ¶ They get	410–11
them off, and turns	388	them off and turns	411
upside down and makes	388	upside down, and makes	412
day time! And I'll	391	daytime! ¶ And I'll	415–16
seen her! I can	392	seen her! ¶ I can	416–17
windows! It is	392	windows! ¶ It is	417–18
she hide under	398	she hides under	423
vines. I don't	398	vines. ¶ I don't	423–24
by daylight! I always	399	by daylight! ¶ I always	425–26
at once. And John	401	at once. ¶ And John	427–28
queer now that	401	queer now, that	428
room! ¶ Besides I don't	402–3	room! Besides, I don't	429
at once. But turn	404	at once. ¶ But, turn	431–32
I can I can	405	I can, I can	432
see her she <u>may</u>	406	see her, she *may*	433
to notice. ¶ I don't	415–16	to notice. I don't	442
his eyes. And I	416	his eyes. ¶ And I	442–43
daytime. John knows	418	daytime. ¶ John knows	445–46
so quiet. He asked	419	so quiet! ¶ He asked	446–47
and kind. As if	420	and kind. ¶ As if	448–49
Still I don't	421	Still, I don't	450
in town overnight	425	in town over night	453
as my head, and half	433	as my head and half	462
laugh at me I declared	434	laugh at me, I declared	463

MS	Line/s	NEM	Line/s
finish it today!	435	finish it to-day!	464
go away tomorrow	436	go away to-morrow	465
get tired. How she	441	get tired. ¶ How she	470–71
that time! But I	441	that time! ¶ But I	471–72
but me—not <u>alive</u>!	442	but me,—not *alive!*	472
when I woke!	445	when I woke.	475
bedstead, nailed	447	bedstead nailed	477
down stairs tonight	448	downstairs to-night	479
home tommorrow	448	home to-morrow	479
room now it	449	room, now it	480
about here! This bedstead	450	about here! ¶ This bedstead	481–82
gnawed! But I	450	gnawed! ¶ But I	482–83
come in until John	453	come in, till John	485
John comes. I want	454	John comes. ¶ I want	486–87
I couldn't reach	457	I could not reach	490
stand on! The bed	457	stand on! ¶ This bed	490–91
<u>not</u> move. I tried	458	*not* move! ¶ I tried	491–92
sticks horribly. And the	461	sticks horribly and the	495
enjoys it. All	461	enjoys it! All	495
wouldn't do it of course! I	465	wouldn't do it. Of course not. I	499
of that wall paper	469	of that wall-paper	503
as I did? But I	469	as I did? ¶ But I	503–4
me to. For outside	474	me to. ¶ For outside	509–10
so I can not	477	so I cannot	513
call and pound?	480	call and pound!	516
for an ax!	481	for an axe.	517
gentlest voice—"The	483	gentlest voice, "the	519
plantain leaf."	484	plantain leaf!"	520
quietly indeed—"Open	486	quietly indeed, "Open	522
"I can't," said I, "The	487	"I can't," said I. "The	523
gently and slowly. ¶ I said it	488–89	gently and slowly, and said it	524
came in. ¶ He stopped	490–91	came in. He stopped	525
the matter!" he cried	491	the matter?" he cried	527
sake what are	492	sake, what are	527
over my shoulder:	493	over my shoulder.	528
you and Jane!	494	you and Jane?	529
fainted? ¶ But he did	496–97	fainted? But he did	531

Editorial Emendations
to the Copy-Texts

THE TEXTS in this edition differ from the original sources only in cases of un-equivocal error. For example, no attempt has been made to supply missing commas where they would "clarify" the sense of a passage, according to the possibility that, if the author intended to represent a rambling thought, the introduction of a pause would *alter*, rather than merely clarify, the sense. No attempts at regulari-zation (making all spellings of "wall-paper," "wallpaper," and "wall paper" con-sistent, for example) or modernization have been made, so as not to unduly affect the observations of students and scholars using the edition.

A note on inconsistent uses of "wall-paper": Line 201 of the *NEM* text begins with an extraneous open quote ("), which was probably meant to temporarily mark the beginning of a new "take"—a section of the manuscript that a second compositor would have set into type. This line appears as the first complete sen-tence on Gilman's original MS page 19 of 58. The word "wall-paper" has been consistently hyphenated in *NEM* until line 194, and its next appearances (begin-ning with line 212) are altered to "wallpaper," sure evidence of a new typesetter. Somewhere between line 335 ("wallpaper") and line 446 ("wall-paper," correspon-ding to MS page 40), a third compositor, or perhaps the first one who preferred hyphens, took up the last twenty or so pages of manuscript to set. The inconsis-tent usage in *NEM* is thus not technically in error, but instead evidence of the col-laborative print-processes of the time, and has not been editorially regularized in this edition.

Gilman's manuscript also contains what appear, on the surface, to be carelessly inconsistent usages. No other explanation that attributes conscious purpose has been devised as above; but that does not mean one cannot be discovered in the fu-ture. For that reason, Gilman's usages have not been regularized either.

All original copy-text errata are recoverable from the following lists.

MS Text	Line	Original
all the time."	60	all the time".
nervousness.	91	nervous.
rental."	105	rental.
else	194	eles
more,"	271	more"?
darling,"	284	darling",
developments	350	developements
creeps	359	creep
hides	398	hide
tomorrow	448	tommorrow
pound!	480	pound?
can't,"	487	can't",
leaf."	487	leaf".

★   ★   ★   ★

NEM text	Line	Original
as airy and comfortable a room	118	an airy and comfortable room
breadths	144	breaths
But	163	"But
It is	201	It it
has not	202	has nos
grotesques	221	grotesque
behind that	330	behind, that
furniture	396	furnitnre
John is to	453	John to
plantain	520	plaintain
Jane!	529	Jane?

The Yellow Wall-Paper Parallel Texts

The Yellow Wall-Paper.

It is very seldom that mere ordinary people like John and I secure ancestral halls for the summer.

A colonial mansion, a hereditary estate, I would say a haunted house, and reach the height of romantic felicity—but that would be asking too much of fate!

Still I will proudly declare that there is <u>something</u> queer about it. Else why should it be let so cheaply? And why have stood so long untenanted?

John laughs at me of course, but one expects that in marriage.

John is practical in the extreme.

He has no patience with faith, an intense horror of superstition, and he scoffs openly at any talk of things not to be felt and seen and put down in figures.

John is a physician, and <u>perhaps</u>,—I wouldn't say it to a living soul of course, but this is dead paper, and a great relief to my mind,—<u>perhaps</u> that is one reason I do not get well faster.

You see he does not believe I am sick! And what can one do? If a physician of high standing, and one's own husband, assures friends and relatives that there is really nothing the matter with one but temporary nervous depression,—a slight hysterical tendency,—what is one to do? My brother is also a physician and also of high standing, and he says the same thing.

So I take phosphates or phosphites—whichever it is, and tonics, and journeys, and air, and exercise, and am absolutely forbidden to "work" until I am well again.

[*NEW ENGLAND MAGAZINE* TEXT, JANUARY 1892]

The Yellow Wall-Paper.

By *Charlotte Perkins Stetson.*

It is very seldom that mere ordinary people like John and myself secure ances- 1
tral halls for the summer.

A colonial mansion, a hereditary estate, I would say a haunted house, and
reach the height of romantic felicity—but that would be asking too much of fate!

Still I will proudly declare that there is something queer about it. 5

Else, why should it be let so cheaply? And why have stood so long untenanted?

John laughs at me, of course, but one expects that in marriage.

John is practical in the extreme. He has no patience with faith, an intense
horror of superstition, and he scoffs openly at any talk of things not to be felt and 10
seen and put down in figures.

John is a physician, and *perhaps*—(I would not say it to a living soul, of
course, but this is dead paper and a great relief to my mind—) *perhaps* that is
one reason I do not get well faster.

You see he does not believe I am sick! 15

And what can one do?

If a physician of high standing, and one's own husband, assures friends and
relatives that there is really nothing the matter with one but temporary nervous
depression—a slight hysterical tendency—what is one to do?

My brother is also a physician, and also of high standing, and he says the 20
same thing.

So I take phosphates or phosphites—whichever it is, and tonics, and journeys, and air, and exercise, and am absolutely forbidden to "work" until I am
well again.

Personally, I disagree with their ideas.

Personally, I believe that congenial work with excitement and change would do me good.

But what is one to do?

I did write for a while in spite of them; but it <u>does</u> exhaust me a good deal, —having to be so sly about it, or else meet heavy opposition.

I sometimes fancy that in my condition if I had less opposition and more society and stimulus—but John says the very worst thing I can do is to think about my condition, and I confess it always makes me feel badly.

So I will let it alone, and write about the house.

The most beautiful place!

It is quite alone, standing well back from the road, and quite three miles from the village. It makes me think of English places that you read about, for there are hedges, and walls, and gates that lock, and lots of separate little houses for the gardeners and people.

There is a <u>delicious</u> garden. I never saw such a garden, large and shady, full of box-bordered paths, and lined with long grape-covered arbors with seats under them.

There were greenhouses too, but they are all broken now.

There was some legal trouble, I believe, something about the heirs and co-heirs; anyhow, it has been empty for years and years.

That spoils my ghostliness, I am afraid, but I don't care—there <u>is</u> something strange about the house—I can feel it. I even said so to John one moonlit evening, but he said what I felt was a <u>draught</u>, and shut the window.

I get unreasonably angry with John sometimes. I'm sure I never used to be so sensitive. I think it is due to this nervous condition.

But John says if I feel so I shall neglect proper self-control; so I take pains to control myself—before him at least, and that makes me very tired.

I don't like our room a bit. I wanted one downstairs, that opened on the piazza and had roses all over the windows, and such pretty old-fashioned chintz hangings; but John wouldn't hear of it.

He said there was only one window and not room for two beds, and no near room for him if he took another.

He is very careful and loving, hardly lets me stir without special direction;

Personally, I disagree with their ideas.

Personally, I believe that congenial work, with excitement and change, would do me good.

But what is one to do?

I did write for a while in spite of them; but it *does* exhaust me a good deal—having to be so sly about it, or else meet with heavy opposition.

I sometimes fancy that in my condition if I had less opposition and more society and stimulus—but John says the very worst thing I can do is to think about my condition, and I confess it always makes me feel bad.

So I will let it alone and talk about the house.

The most beautiful place! It is quite alone, standing well back from the road, quite three miles from the village. It makes me think of English places that you read about, for there are hedges and walls and gates that lock, and lots of separate little houses for the gardeners and people.

There is a *delicious* garden! I never saw such a garden—large and shady, full of box-bordered paths, and lined with long grape-covered arbors with seats under them.

There were greenhouses, too, but they are all broken now.

There was some legal trouble, I believe, something about the heirs and co-heirs; anyhow, the place has been empty for years.

That spoils my ghostliness, I am afraid, but I don't care—there is something strange about the house—I can feel it.

I even said so to John one moonlight evening, but he said what I felt was a *draught*, and shut the window.

I get unreasonably angry with John sometimes. I'm sure I never used to be so sensitive. I think it is due to this nervous condition.

But John says if I feel so, I shall neglect proper self-control; so I take pains to control myself—before him, at least, and that makes me very tired.

I don't like our room a bit. I wanted one downstairs that opened on the pi-azza and had roses all over the window, and such pretty old-fashioned chintz hangings! but John would not hear of it.

He said there was only one window and not room for two beds, and no near room for him if he took another.

He is very careful and loving, and hardly lets me stir without special direction.

I have a schedule prescription for each hour in the day, he takes every care, and I feel basely ungrateful not to value it more. He said we came here solely on my account, that I was to have perfect rest, and all the air I could get. "Your exercise depends on your strength my dear" said he, "and your food somewhat on your appetite; but air you can absorb all the time."

So we took the nursery at the top of the house.

It is a big airy room, the whole floor nearly, with windows that look all ways, and air and sunlight galore. It was nursery first, and then playroom and gymnasium, I should judge, for the windows are barred for little children and there are rings and things in the walls. The paint and paper look as if a boy's school had used it. It is stripped off—the paper—in great patches, all around the head of my bed about as far as I can reach, and in a great place on the other side of the room, low down.

I never saw a worse paper in my life. One of those sprawling, flamboyant patterns, committing every artistic sin. It is dull enough to confuse the eye in following, pronounced enough to constantly irritate and provoke study, and when you follow the lame uncertain curves for a little distance they suddenly commit suicide—plunge off at outrageous angles, destroy themselves in unheard of contradictions.

The color is repellant, almost revolting; a smouldering unclean yellow, strangely faded by the slow-turning sun. It is a dull yet lurid orange in some places, a sickly sulphur tint in others.

No wonder the children hated it! I should hate it myself if I had to live in this room long.

There comes John, and I must put this away—he hates to have me write a word.

+   +   +   . +

We have been here two weeks, and I haven't felt like writing before since that first day.

I am sitting by the window now, up in this atrocious nursery, and there is nothing to hinder my writing as much as I please, save lack of strength.

John is away all day, and even some nights when his cases are serious. I am glad my case is not serious.

But these nervous troubles are dreadfully depressing.

I have a schedule prescription for each hour in the day; he takes all care 60 from me, and so I feel basely ungrateful not to value it more.

He said we came here solely on my account, that I was to have perfect rest and all the air I could get. "Your exercise depends on your strength, my dear," said he, "and your food somewhat on your appetite; but air you can absorb all the time." So we took the nursery at the top of the house. 65

It is a big, airy room, the whole floor nearly, with windows that look all ways, and air and sunshine galore. It was nursery first and then playroom and gymnasium, I should judge; for the windows are barred for little children, and there are rings and things in the walls.

The paint and paper look as if a boys' school had used it. It is stripped off— 70 the paper—in great patches all around the head of my bed, about as far as I can reach, and in a great place on the other side of the room low down. I never saw a worse paper in my life.

One of those sprawling flamboyant patterns committing every artistic sin.

It is dull enough to confuse the eye in following, pronounced enough to 75 constantly irritate and provoke study, and when you follow the lame uncertain curves for a little distance they suddenly commit suicide—plunge off at outrageous angles, destroy themselves in unheard of contradictions.

The color is repellant, almost revolting; a smouldering unclean yellow, strangely faded by the slow-turning sunlight. 80

It is a dull yet lurid orange in some places, a sickly sulphur tint in others.

No wonder the children hated it! I should hate it myself if I had to live in this room long.

There comes John, and I must put this away,—he hates to have me write a word. 85

            ★   ★   ★   ★   ★   ★

We have been here two weeks, and I haven't felt like writing before, since that first day.

I am sitting by the window now, up in this atrocious nursery, and there is nothing to hinder my writing as much as I please, save lack of strength. 90

John is away all day, and even some nights when his cases are serious.

I am glad my case is not serious!

But these nervous troubles are dreadfully depressing.

90　　John doesn't know how much I really suffer. He knows there is no <u>reason</u> to suffer, and that satisfies him. Of course it is only nervousness. It does weigh on me so not to do my duty in any way. I meant to be such a help to John, such a real rest and comfort, and here I am a comparative burden already! Nobody would believe what an effort it is just to do what little I am able. To dress and
95　　entertain and order things. It is fortunate Mary is so good with the baby. Such a dear baby!

And yet I can <u>not</u> be with him, it makes me so nervous.

I suppose John was never nervous in his life. He laughs at me so about this wallpaper! At first he meant to re-paper the room, but afterwards he said that
100　　I was letting it get the better of me, and that nothing was worse for a nervous patient than to give way to such fancies. He said that after the wallpaper was changed it would be the heavy bedstead, and then the barred windows, and then that gate at the head of the stairs, and so on. "You know the place is doing you good" he said, "and really, dear, I don't care to renovate the house just for
105　　a three months rental."

"Then do let us go down stairs" I said, "there are such pretty rooms there!"

Then he took me in his arms and called me a blessed little goose, and said he would go down cellar if I wished, and have it white-washed into the bargain!

But he is right enough about the beds and windows and things. It <u>is</u> as airy
110　　and comfortable a room as anyone need wish, and of course I wouldn't be so silly as to make him uncomfortable just for a whim.

I'm really getting quite fond of the big room, all but that horrid paper.

Out of one window I can see the garden, those mysterious deep-shaded arbors, the riotous oldfashioned flowers and bushes, the gnarly trees. Out of an-
115　　other I get a lovely view of the bay and a little private wharf that belongs to the estate. There is a beautiful shaded lane that runs down there from the house. I always fancy I see people walking in these numerous paths and arbors, but John has cautioned me not to give way to fancy in the least. He says that with my imaginative power and habit of story making, a nervous weakness like mine is
120　　sure to lead to all manner of excited fancies, and that I ought to use my will and good sense to check the tendency. So I try.

John does not know how much I really suffer. He knows there is no *reason* to suffer, and that satisfies him.

Of course it is only nervousness. It does weigh on me so not to do my duty in any way!

I meant to be such a help to John, such a real rest and comfort, and here I am a comparative burden already!

Nobody would believe what an effort it is to do what little I am able,—to dress and entertain, and order things.

It is fortunate Mary is so good with the baby. Such a dear baby!

And yet I *cannot* be with him, it makes me so nervous.

I suppose John never was nervous in his life. He laughs at me so about this wall-paper!

At first he meant to repaper the room, but afterwards he said that I was letting it get the better of me, and that nothing was worse for a nervous patient than to give way to such fancies.

He said that after the wall-paper was changed it would be the heavy bedstead, and then the barred windows, and then that gate at the head of the stairs, and so on.

"You know the place is doing you good," he said, "and really, dear, I don't care to renovate the house just for a three months' rental."

"Then do let us go downstairs," I said, "there are such pretty rooms there."

Then he took me in his arms and called me a blessed little goose, and said he would go down cellar, if I wished, and have it whitewashed into the bargain.

But he is right enough about the beds and windows and things.

It is as airy and comfortable a room as any one need wish, and, of course, I would not be so silly as to make him uncomfortable just for a whim.

I'm really getting quite fond of the big room, all but that horrid paper.

Out of one window I can see the garden, those mysterious deep-shaded arbors, the riotous old-fashioned flowers, and bushes and gnarly trees.

Out of another I get a lovely view of the bay and a little private wharf belonging to the estate. There is a beautiful shaded lane that runs down there from the house. I always fancy I see people walking in these numerous paths and arbors, but John has cautioned me not to give way to fancy in the least. He says that with my imaginative power and habit of story-making, a nervous weakness like mine is sure to lead to all manner of excited fancies, and that I ought to use my will and good sense to check the tendency. So I try.

I think sometimes that if I were only well enough to write a little it would relieve the pressure of ideas and rest me.

But I find I get pretty tired when I try. It is so discouraging not to have any advice and companionship about my work. When I get really well John says we will ask Cousin Henry and Julia down for a long visit; but he says he would as soon put fireworks in my pillowcase as to let me have those stimulating people about now. I wish I could get well faster. But I mustn't think about that.

This paper looks to me as if it <u>knew</u> what a vicious influence it had!

There is a recurrent spot where the pattern lolls like a broken neck, and two bulbous eyes stare at you upside down.

I get positively angry with the impertinence of it, and the everlastingness. Up and down and sideways they crawl, and those absurd unblinking eyes are everywhere. There is one place where two breadths didn't match, and the eyes go all up and down the line, one a little higher than the other. I never saw so much expression in an inanimate thing before, and we all know how much expression inanimate things have! I used to lie awake as a child, and get more entertainment and terror out of blank walls and plain furniture than most children could find in a toystore. I remember what a kindly wink the knobs of our big old bureau used to have; and there was one chair that always seemed like a strong friend. I used to feel that if any of the other things looked too fierce I could always hop into that chair and be safe.

The furniture in this room is no worse than inharmonious, however, for we had to bring it all from down stairs. I suppose when this was used as a play room they had to take the nursery things out—and no wonder! for I never saw such ravages as the children have made here.

The wall-paper, as I said before, is torn off in spots, and it sticketh closer than a brother—they must have had perseverance as well as hatred. Then the floor is scratched and gouged and splintered, the plaster itself is dug out here and there, and this great heavy bed which is all we found in the room, looks as if it had been through the wars. But I don't mind it a bit—only the paper.

I think sometimes that if I were only well enough to write a little it would   130
relieve the press of ideas and rest me.

But I find I get pretty tired when I try.

It is so discouraging not to have any advice and companionship about my
work. When I get really well, John says we will ask Cousin Henry and Julia
down for a long visit; but he says he would as soon put fireworks in my pillow-   135
case as to let me have those stimulating people about now.

I wish I could get well faster.

But I must not think about that. This paper looks to me as if it *knew* what
a vicious influence it had!

There is a recurrent spot where the pattern lolls like a broken neck and two   140
bulbous eyes stare at you upside down.

I get positively angry with the impertinence of it and the everlastingness. Up
and down and sideways they crawl, and those absurd, unblinking eyes are everywhere. There is one place where two breadths didn't match, and the eyes go all
up and down the line, one a little higher than the other.   145

I never saw so much expression in an inanimate thing before, and we all
know how much expression they have! I used to lie awake as a child and get more
entertainment and terror out of blank walls and plain furniture than most children could find in a toy-store.

I remember what a kindly wink the knobs of our big, old bureau used to   150
have, and there was one chair that always seemed like a strong friend.

I used to feel that if any of the other things looked too fierce I could always
hop into that chair and be safe.

The furniture in this room is no worse than inharmonious, however, for
we had to bring it all from downstairs. I suppose when this was used as a play-   155
room they had to take the nursery things out, and no wonder! I never saw such
ravages as the children have made here.

The wall-paper, as I said before, is torn off in spots, and it sticketh closer
than a brother—they must have had perseverance as well as hatred.

Then the floor is scratched and gouged and splintered, the plaster itself is   160
dug out here and there, and this great heavy bed which is all we found in the
room, looks as if it had been through the wars.

But I don't mind it a bit—only the paper.

There comes John's sister—such a dear girl as she is, and so careful of me! I mustn't let her find me writing.

She is a perfect—,an enthusiastic—,housekeeper, and hopes for no better profession. I verily believe she thinks it is the writing which made me sick!

But I can write when she is out, and see her a long way off, from these windows.

There is one that commands the road, a lovely shaded winding road; and one that just looks off over the country. A lovely country too, full of great elms and velvet meadows.

This wall paper has a kind of subpattern in a different shade, a particularly irritating one, for you can only see it in certain lights, and not clearly then. But in the places where it isn't faded, and when the sun is just so,—I can see a strange provoking formless sort of figure, that seems to skulk about behind that silly and conspicuous front design.

There's sister on the stairs!

+   +   +   +

Well, the Fourth of July is over! The people are all gone and I am tired out.

John thought it might do me good to see a little company, so we just had Mother and Nellie and the children down for a week.

Of course I didn't do a thing—Jennie sees to everything now. But it tired me all the same. John says if I don't pick up faster he shall send me to Weir Mitchell in the Fall.

But I don't want to go there at all. I had a friend who was in his hands once, and she says he is just like John and my brother only more so!

Besides it is such an undertaking to go so far. I don't feel as if it were worth while to turn my hand over for anything, and I'm getting dreadfully fretful and querulous. I cry at nothing and cry most of the time. Of course I don't when John is here, or anybody else, but when I am alone.

And I am alone a good deal just now. John is kept in town very often by serious cases, and Jennie is good and lets me alone when I want her to. So I walk a little in the garden or down that lovely lane, sit on the porch under the roses, and lie down up here a good deal.

There comes John's sister. Such a dear girl as she is, and so careful of me! I must not let her find me writing.

She is a perfect and enthusiastic housekeeper, and hopes for no better profession. I verily believe she thinks it is the writing which made me sick!

But I can write when she is out, and see her a long way off from these windows.

There is one that commands the road, a lovely shaded winding road, and one that just looks off over the country. A lovely country, too, full of great elms and velvet meadows.

This wallpaper has a kind of sub-pattern in a different shade, a particularly irritating one, for you can only see it in certain lights, and not clearly then.

But in the places where it isn't faded and where the sun is just so—I can see a strange, provoking, formless sort of figure, that seems to skulk about behind that silly and conspicuous front design.

There's sister on the stairs!

*   *   *   *   *   *

Well, the Fourth of July is over! The people are all gone and I am tired out. John thought it might do me good to see a little company, so we just had mother and Nellie and the children down for a week.

Of course I didn't do a thing. Jennie sees to everything now.

But it tired me all the same.

John says if I don't pick up faster he shall send me to Weir Mitchell in the fall.

But I don't want to go there at all. I had a friend who was in his hands once, and she says he is just like John and my brother, only more so!

Besides, it is such an undertaking to go so far.

I don't feel as if it was worth while to turn my hand over for anything, and I'm getting dreadfully fretful and querulous.

I cry at nothing, and cry most of the time.

Of course I don't when John is here, or anybody else, but when I am alone.

And I am alone a good deal just now. John is kept in town very often by serious cases, and Jennie is good and lets me alone when I want her to.

So I walk a little in the garden or down that lovely lane, sit on the porch under the roses, and lie down up here a good deal.

I'm getting really fond of the room in spite of the wall-paper.

185 Perhaps <u>because</u> of the wall-paper! It dwells in my mind so! I lie here on this great immovable bed (—it's nailed down, I believe!) and follow that pattern about by the hour.

It is as good as gymnastics, I assure you. I start, we'll say, at the bottom, down in the corner over there where it hasn't been touched; and I determine,

190 for the thousandth time, that I <u>will</u> follow that pointless pattern to some sort of a conclusion.

I know a little of the principles of design, and I know this thing was not arranged on any laws of radiation, or alternation, or repetition, or symmetry, or anything else that I ever heard of. It is repeated of course, by the breadth,

195 but not otherwise.

Looked at in one way each breadth stands alone, the bloated curves and flourishes—a kind of debased Romanesque with <u>delirium tremens</u>—go waddling up and down in isolated columns of fatuity.

But on the other hand they connect diagonally, and the sprawling outlines

200 run off in great slanting waves of optic horror; like a lot of wallowing sea-weeds in full chase.

The whole thing goes horizontally, too, at least it seems so, and I exhaust myself in trying to distinguish the order of its going in that direction. They have used a horizontal breadth for a border, and that adds wonderfully to the

205 confusion.

There is one end of the room where it is almost intact, and there, when the cross-lights fade and the low sun shines directly on it, I can almost fancy radiation after all; the interminable grotesques seem to form around a common center and rush off in headlong plunges of equal distraction.

210 It makes me tired to follow it. I will take a nap I guess.

+   +   +   +

I don't know why I should write this.

I don't want to.

I don't feel able.

215 And I know John would think it absurd. But I <u>must</u> say what I feel and think in some way—it is such a relief.

But the effort is getting to be greater than the relief.

I'm getting really fond of the room in spite of the wallpaper. Perhaps *because* of the wallpaper.

It dwells in my mind so!

I lie here on this great immovable bed—it is nailed down, I believe—and follow that pattern about by the hour. It is as good as gymnastics, I assure you. I start, we'll say, at the bottom, down in the corner over there where it has not been touched, and I determine for the thousandth time that I *will* follow that pointless pattern to some sort of a conclusion.

I know a little of the principle of design, and I know this thing was not arranged on any laws of radiation, or alternation, or repetition, or symmetry, or anything else that I ever heard of.

It is repeated, of course, by the breadths, but not otherwise.

Looked at in one way each breadth stands alone, the bloated curves and flourishes—a kind of "debased Romanesque" with *delirium tremens*—go waddling up and down in isolated columns of fatuity.

But, on the other hand, they connect diagonally, and the sprawling outlines run off in great slanting waves of optic horror, like a lot of wallowing seaweeds in full chase.

The whole thing goes horizontally, too, at least it seems so, and I exhaust myself in trying to distinguish the order of its going in that direction.

They have used a horizontal breadth for a frieze, and that adds wonderfully to the confusion.

There is one end of the room where it is almost intact, and there, when the crosslights fade and the low sun shines directly upon it, I can almost fancy radiation after all,—the interminable grotesques seem to form around a common centre and rush off in headlong plunges of equal distraction.

It makes me tired to follow it. I will take a nap I guess.

★   ★   ★   ★   ★   ★

I don't know why I should write this.

I don't want to.

I don't feel able.

And I know John would think it absurd. But I *must* say what I feel and think in some way—it is such a relief!

But the effort is getting to be greater than the relief.

Half the time now I am lazy, awfully lazy, and lie down ever so much. John says I mustn't lose my strength, and has me take codliver-oil and lots of tonics and things, to say nothing of ale and wine and rare meat.

Dear John! He loves me very dearly, and hates to have me sick. I tried to have a real earnest reasonable talk with him the other day, and tell him how I wish he would let me go and make a visit to Cousin Henry and Julia. But he said I wasn't able to go, nor able to stand it after I got there; and I did not make out a very good case for myself, for I was crying before I had finished.

It is getting to be a great effort for me to think straight—just this nervous weakness, I suppose.

And dear John gathered me up in his strong arms and just carried me up stairs and laid me on the bed, and sat by me, and read to me till it tired my head.

He said I was his darling, and his comfort, and all he had, and that I must take care of myself for his sake, and keep well. He says no one but myself can help me out of it, that I must use my will and self-control and not let any silly fancies run away with me.

There's <u>one</u> comfort, the baby is well and happy, and does not have to occupy this nursery with the horrid wall-paper. If I had not used it that blessed child would have!

What a fortunate escape!

Why, I wouldn't have a child of mine, an impressionable little thing, live in such a room for worlds.

I never thought of it before, but it is lucky that John kept me here after all.

I can stand it so much easier than a baby you see! Of course I never mention it to them any more—I am too wise, but I keep watch of it all the same. There are things in that paper that nobody knows but me, or ever will. Behind that outside pattern the dim shapes get clearer every day. It is always the same shape, only very numerous. And it's like a woman stooping down, and creeping about behind that pattern. I don't like it a bit. I wonder—I begin to think—.

I wish John would take me from here!—

It is so hard to talk with John about my case, because he is so wise, and because he loves me so.

But I tried it last night.

It was moonlight. The moon shines in all round just as the sun does.

Half the time now I am awfully lazy, and lie down ever so much.

John says I mustn't lose my strength, and has me take cod liver oil and lots of tonics and things, to say nothing of ale and wine and rare meat.

Dear John! He loves me very dearly, and hates to have me sick. I tried to have a real earnest reasonable talk with him the other day, and tell him how I wish he would let me go and make a visit to Cousin Henry and Julia.

But he said I wasn't able to go, nor able to stand it after I got there; and I did not make out a very good case for myself, for I was crying before I had finished.

It is getting to be a great effort for me to think straight. Just this nervous weakness I suppose.

And dear John gathered me up in his arms, and just carried me upstairs and laid me on the bed, and sat by me and read to me till it tired my head.

He said I was his darling and his comfort and all he had, and that I must take care of myself for his sake, and keep well.

He says no one but myself can help me out of it, that I must use my will and self-control and not let any silly fancies run away with me.

There's one comfort, the baby is well and happy, and does not have to occupy this nursery with the horrid wallpaper.

If we had not used it, that blessed child would have! What a fortunate escape! Why, I wouldn't have a child of mine, an impressionable little thing, live in such a room for worlds.

I never thought of it before, but it is lucky that John kept me here after all, I can stand it so much easier than a baby, you see.

Of course I never mention it to them any more—I am too wise,—but I keep watch of it all the same.

There are things in that paper that nobody knows but me, or ever will.

Behind that outside pattern the dim shapes get clearer every day.

It is always the same shape, only very numerous.

And it is like a woman stooping down and creeping about behind that pattern. I don't like it a bit. I wonder—I begin to think—I wish John would take me away from here!

*   *   *   *   *   *

It is so hard to talk with John about my case, because he is so wise, and because he loves me so.

But I tried it last night.

It was moonlight. The moon shines in all around just as the sun does.

I hate to see it sometimes, it creeps so slowly, and always comes in by one window or another.

255 John was asleep and I hated to waken him, so I kept still and watched the moonlight on that undulating wall-paper till it made me creepy.

The faint figure behind seemed to shake the pattern, just as if she wanted to get out.

I got up softly and went to feel and see if the paper <u>did</u> move, and when I 260 came back John was awake.

"What is it little girl?" he said. "Don't go walking about like that—you'll get cold."

I thought it was a good time to talk, so I told him that I really was not gaining here, and that I wished he would take me away.

265 "Why, darling," said he, "our lease will be up in three weeks, and I can't see how to leave before. The repairs are not done at home, and I can't possibly leave town just now. Of course if you were in any danger I could and would, but you really are better, dear, whether you can see it or not. I am a doctor, dear, and I know. You are gaining flesh and color, your appetite is better, I feel really much 270 easier about you."

"I don't weigh a bit more," said I, "nor as much; and my appetite may be better in the evening when you are here, but it is worse in the morning when you are away."

"Bless her little heart!" said he, with a big hug, "she shall be as sick as she 275 pleases! But now let's improve the shining hours by going to sleep, and talk about it in the morning!"

"And you won't go away?" I asked gloomily.

"Why, how can I, dear? It is only three weeks more and then we will take a nice little trip of a few days while Jennie is getting the house ready. Really, dear, 280 you are better!"

"Better in <u>body</u>, perhaps"—I began, and stopped short; for he sat up straight and looked at me with such a stern reproachful look that I could not say another word.

"My darling," said he, "I beg of you, for my sake and our child's sake, as well 285 as for your own, that you will never for one instant let <u>that</u> idea enter your mind. There is nothing so dangerous, so fascinating, to a temperament like yours. It is a false and foolish fancy. Can you not trust me as a physician when I tell you so?"

I hate to see it sometimes, it creeps so slowly, and always comes in by one window or another.

John was asleep and I hated to waken him, so I kept still and watched the moonlight on that undulating wallpaper till I felt creepy.

The faint figure behind seemed to shake the pattern, just as if she wanted to get out.

I got up softly and went to feel and see if the paper *did* move, and when I came back John was awake.

"What is it, little girl?" he said. "Don't go walking about like that—you'll get cold."

I thought it was a good time to talk, so I told him that I really was not gaining here, and that I wished he would take me away.

"Why, darling!" said he, "our lease will be up in three weeks, and I can't see how to leave before.

"The repairs are not done at home, and I cannot possibly leave town just now. Of course if you were in any danger, I could and would, but you really are better, dear, whether you can see it or not. I am a doctor, dear, and I know. You are gaining flesh and color, your appetite is better, I feel really much easier about you."

"I don't weigh a bit more," said I, "nor as much; and my appetite may be better in the evening when you are here, but it is worse in the morning when you are away!"

"Bless her little heart!" said he with a big hug, "she shall be as sick as she pleases! But now let's improve the shining hours by going to sleep, and talk about it in the morning!"

"And you won't go away?" I asked gloomily.

"Why, how can I, dear? It is only three weeks more and then we will take a nice little trip of a few days while Jennie is getting the house ready. Really dear you are better!"

"Better in body perhaps—" I began, and stopped short, for he sat up straight and looked at me with such a stern, reproachful look that I could not say another word.

"My darling," said he, "I beg of you, for my sake and for our child's sake, as well as for your own, that you will never for one instant let that idea enter your mind! There is nothing so dangerous, so fascinating, to a temperament like yours. It is a false and foolish fancy. Can you not trust me as a physician when I tell you so?"

270

275

280

285

290

295

300

So of course I said no more on that score, and he went to sleep before long.

He thought I was asleep first, but I wasn't. I lay there for hours trying to decide whether the front pattern and the back pattern really did move together or separately.

+   +   +   +

In a pattern like this, by daylight, there is a certain lack of sequence, a defiance of law that is a constant irritant to a normal mind.

The color is hideous enough, and unreliable enough, and infuriating enough; but the pattern is torturing.

You think you have mastered it, but just as you get well underway in following it it turns a back somersault and there you are! It slaps you in the face, knocks you down and tramples on you. It is like a bad dream. The outside pattern is a florid arabesque, reminding one of a fungus. If you can imagine a toadstool in joints, an interminable string of toadstools, budding and sprouting in endless convolutions—why, that is something like it.

That is, <u>sometimes</u>!

There is one marked peculiarity about this paper, a thing nobody seems to notice but myself, and that is that it changes as the light changes.

When the sun shoots in through the east window—I always watch for that first long straight ray—it changes so quickly that I never can quite believe it. That is why I watch it always. By moonlight—the moon shines in all night when there is a moon—I wouldn't know it was the same paper. At night, in any kind of light, in twilight, candlelight, lamplight, and worst of all by moonlight— it becomes <u>bars</u>! The outside pattern, I mean. And the woman behind is as plain as can be.

I didn't realize for a long time what the thing was that showed behind, the dim sub-pattern, but now I am quite sure it is a woman.

By daylight she is subdued,—quiet. I fancy it is the pattern that keeps her so still. It is so puzzling. It keeps <u>me</u> quiet by the hour. I lie down ever so much now. John says it is good for me, and to sleep all I can. Indeed he started the habit—by making me lie down for an hour after each meal. It is a very bad habit I am convinced, for you see I don't sleep!

And that cultivates deceit, for I don't tell <u>them</u> I'm awake—O no!

So of course I said no more on that score, and we went to sleep before long. He thought I was asleep first, but I wasn't, and lay there for hours trying to decide whether that front pattern and the back pattern really did move together or separately.

*   *   *   *   *   *

On a pattern like this, by daylight, there is a lack of sequence, a defiance of law, that is a constant irritant to a normal mind.

The color is hideous enough, and unreliable enough, and infuriating enough, but the pattern is torturing.

You think you have mastered it, but just as you get well underway in following, it turns a back-somersault and there you are. It slaps you in the face, knocks you down, and tramples upon you. It is like a bad dream.

The outside pattern is a florid arabesque, reminding one of a fungus. If you can imagine a toadstool in joints, an interminable string of toadstools, budding and sprouting in endless convolutions—why, that is something like it.

That is, sometimes!

There is one marked peculiarity about this paper, a thing nobody seems to notice but myself, and that is that it changes as the light changes.

When the sun shoots in through the east window—I always watch for that first long, straight ray—it changes so quickly that I never can quite believe it.

That is why I watch it always.

By moonlight—the moon shines in all night when there is a moon—I wouldn't know it was the same paper.

At night in any kind of light, in twilight, candlelight, lamplight, and worst of all by moonlight, it becomes bars! The outside pattern I mean, and the woman behind it is as plain as can be.

I didn't realize for a long time what the thing was that showed behind that dim sub-pattern, but now I am quite sure it is a woman.

By daylight she is subdued, quiet. I fancy it is the pattern that keeps her so still. It is so puzzling. It keeps me quiet by the hour.

I lie down ever so much now. John says it is good for me, and to sleep all I can.

Indeed he started the habit by making me lie down for an hour after each meal.

It is a very bad habit I am convinced, for you see I don't sleep.

And that cultivates deceit, for I don't tell them I'm awake—O no!

The fact is I am getting a little afraid of John. He seems very queer sometimes. And even Jennie has an inexplicable look.

It strikes me occasionally, just as scientific hypothesis,—that perhaps it is the paper!

I have watched John when he didn't know I was looking—and come into the room suddenly on the most innocent excuses, and I've caught him several times <u>looking at the paper</u>! And Jennie, too.

I caught Jennie with her hand on it once.

She didn't know I was in the room, and when I asked her in a quiet, a very quiet voice, with the most restrained manner possible, what she was doing with the paper? she turned around as if she had been caught stealing and looked quite angry—asked me why I should frighten her so!

Then she said that the paper stained everything it touched, that she had found yellow smooches on all my clothes and John's, and she wished we would be more careful!

Did not that sound innocent? But <u>I</u> know she was studying that pattern, and I am determined that nobody shall find it out but myself!

+   +   +   +

Life is very much more exciting now than it used to be. You see I have something to expect, to look forward to, to watch. I really do eat better, and am much more quiet than I was. John is so pleased to see me improve.

He laughed a little the other day and said I seemed to be flourishing in spite of my wall paper. I turned it off with a laugh. I had no intention of telling him it was <u>because</u> of the wall-paper!

He would make fun of me. He might even take me away. I don't want to leave now until I have found it out. There is a week more, and I think that will be enough.

+   +   +   +

I'm feeling ever so much better! I don't sleep much at night, for it is so interesting to watch developments, but I sleep a good deal in the daytime. In the daytime it is tiresome and perplexing. There are always new shoots on the fungus, and new shades of yellow all over it. I can <u>not</u> keep count of them, though I have tried conscientiously. It is the strangest yellow—that paper! A sickly penetrating suggestive yellow. It makes me think of all the yellow things I ever saw—not beautiful ones like buttercups, but old foul bad yellow things.

The fact is I am getting a little afraid of John.

He seems very queer sometimes, and even Jennie has an inexplicable look. 340

It strikes me occasionally, just as a scientific hypothesis,—that perhaps it is the paper!

I have watched John when he did not know I was looking, and come into the room suddenly on the most innocent excuses, and I've caught him several times *looking at the paper!* And Jennie too. I caught Jennie with her hand on it once. 345

She didn't know I was in the room, and when I asked her in a quiet, a very quiet voice, with the most restrained manner possible, what she was doing with the paper—she turned around as if she had been caught stealing, and looked quite angry—asked me why I should frighten her so!

Then she said that the paper stained everything it touched, that she had 350 found yellow smooches on all my clothes and John's, and she wished we would be more careful!

Did not that sound innocent? But I know she was studying that pattern, and I am determined that nobody shall find it out but myself!

*   *   *   *   *   * 355

Life is very much more exciting now than it used to be. You see I have something more to expect, to look forward to, to watch. I really do eat better, and am more quiet than I was.

John is so pleased to see me improve! He laughed a little the other day, and said I seemed to be flourishing in spite of my wall-paper. 360

I turned it off with a laugh. I had no intention of telling him it was *because* of the wall-paper—he would make fun of me. He might even want to take me away.

I don't want to leave now until I have found it out. There is a week more, and I think that will be enough. 365

*   *   *   *   *   *

I'm feeling ever so much better! I don't sleep much at night, for it is so interesting to watch developments; but I sleep a good deal in the daytime.

In the daytime it is tiresome and perplexing.

There are always new shoots on the fungus, and new shades of yellow all 370 over it. I cannot keep count of them, though I have tried conscientiously.

It is the strangest yellow, that wall-paper! It makes me think of all the yellow things I ever saw—not beautiful ones like buttercups, but old foul, bad yellow things.

But there is another thing about that paper—the smell!

I noticed it the moment we came into the room, but with so much air and sun it was not bad. Now we have had a week of fog and rain, and whether the windows are open or not the smell is here. It creeps all over the house. I find it hovering in the dining room, skulking in the parlor, hiding in the hall, lying in wait for me on the stairs. It gets into my hair. Even when I go to ride, if I turn my head suddenly and surprise it there is that smell!

Such a peculiar odor too! I have spent hours in trying to analyze it, to find what it smelled like. It is not bad—at first, and very gentle, but quite the subtlest, most enduring odor I ever met.

In this damp weather it is awful. I wake up in the night and find it hanging over me. It used to disturb me at first. I thought seriously of burning the house to reach the smell. But now I am used to it. The only thing I can think of that it is like is the <u>color</u> of the paper! A yellow smell.

There is a very funny mark on this wall, low down, near the mop-board. A streak that runs all round the room.

It goes behind every piece of furniture except the bed; a long straight even smooch, as if it had been rubbed over and over.

I wonder how it was done, and who did it, and what they did it for! Round and round and round—round and round and round—it makes me dizzy!

+   +   +   +

I really have discovered something at last. Through watching so much at night, when it changes so, I have finally found out.

The front pattern <u>does</u> move—and no wonder!

The woman behind shakes it! Sometimes I think there are a great many women behind, and sometimes only one and she crawls around fast. And her crawling shakes it all over.

Then in the very bright spots she keeps still, and in very shady spots she just takes hold of the bars and shakes them hard.

But there is something else about that paper—the smell! I noticed it the moment we came into the room, but with so much air and sun it was not bad. Now we have had a week of fog and rain, and whether the windows are open or not, the smell is here.

It creeps all over the house.

I find it hovering in the dining-room, skulking in the parlor, hiding in the hall, lying in wait for me on the stairs.

It gets into my hair.

Even when I go to ride, if I turn my head suddenly and surprise it—there is that smell!

Such a peculiar odor, too! I have spent hours in trying to analyze it, to find what it smelled like.

It is not bad—at first, and very gentle, but quite the subtlest, most enduring odor I ever met.

In this damp weather it is awful, I wake up in the night and find it hanging over me.

It used to disturb me at first. I thought seriously of burning the house—to reach the smell.

But now I am used to it. The only thing I can think of that it is like is the *color* of the paper! A yellow smell.

There is a very funny mark on this wall, low down, near the mopboard. A streak that runs round the room. It goes behind every piece of furniture, except the bed, a long, straight, even *smooch,* as if it had been rubbed over and over.

I wonder how it was done and who did it, and what they did it for. Round and round and round—round and round and round—it makes me dizzy!

*   *   *   *   *   *

I really have discovered something at last.

Through watching so much at night, when it changes so, I have finally found out.

The front pattern *does* move—and no wonder! The woman behind shakes it!

Sometimes I think there are a great many women behind, and sometimes only one, and she crawls around fast, and her crawling shakes it all over.

Then in the very bright spots she keeps still, and in the very shady spots she just takes hold of the bars and shakes them hard.

385 And she is all the time trying to climb through.

But nobody could climb through that pattern, it strangles so. I think that is why it has so many heads. They get through, and then the pattern strangles them off, and turns them upside down and makes their eyes white!

If those heads were covered or taken off it would not be half so bad.

390 +   +   +   +

I think that woman gets out in the day time! And I'll tell you why—privately —I've seen her! I can see her out of every one of my windows! It is the same woman, I know, for she is always creeping, and most women do not creep by daylight.

395 I see her in that long shaded lane, creeping up and down. I see her in those dark grape arbors, creeping all around the garden.

I see her on that long road under the trees, creeping along, and when a carriage comes she hides under the blackberry vines. I don't blame her a bit. It must be very unpleasant to be caught creeping by daylight! I always lock the door

400 when I creep by daylight. I can't do it at night, for I know John would suspect something at once. And John is so queer now that I don't want to irritate him. I wish he would take another room!

Besides I don't want anybody to get that woman out at night but me.

I often wonder if I could see her out of all the windows at once. But turn

405 as fast as I can I can only see out of one at a time.

And though I always see her she <u>may</u> be able to creep faster than I can turn! I have watched her sometimes away off in the open country, creeping as fast as a cloud shadow in a high wind.

+   +   +   +

410 If only that top pattern could be gotten off from the under one! I mean to try tearing it, little by little.

I have found out another funny thing, but I shan't tell it this time! It does not do to trust people too much.

There are only two more days to get this paper off, and I believe John is be-

415 ginning to notice.

I don't like the look in his eyes. And I heard him ask Jennie a lot of professional questions about me. She had a very good report to give.

And she is all the time trying to climb through. But nobody could climb through that pattern—it strangles so; I think that is why it has so many heads.

They get through, and then the pattern strangles them off and turns them upside down, and makes their eyes white!

If those heads were covered or taken off it would not be half so bad.

*   *   *   *   *   *

I think that woman gets out in the daytime!

And I'll tell you why—privately—I've seen her!

I can see her out of every one of my windows!

It is the same woman, I know, for she is always creeping, and most women do not creep by daylight.

I see her in that long shaded lane, creeping up and down. I see her in those dark grape arbors, creeping all around the garden.

I see her on that long road under the trees, creeping along, and when a carriage comes she hides under the blackberry vines.

I don't blame her a bit. It must be very humiliating to be caught creeping by daylight!

I always lock the door when I creep by daylight. I can't do it at night, for I know John would suspect something at once.

And John is so queer now, that I don't want to irritate him. I wish he would take another room! Besides, I don't want anybody to get that woman out at night but myself.

I often wonder if I could see her out of all the windows at once.

But, turn as fast as I can, I can only see out of one at one time.

And though I always see her, she *may* be able to creep faster than I can turn!

I have watched her sometimes away off in the open country, creeping as fast as a cloud shadow in a high wind.

*   *   *   *   *   *

If only that top pattern could be gotten off from the under one! I mean to try it, little by little.

I have found out another funny thing, but I shan't tell it this time! It does not do to trust people too much.

There are only two more days to get this paper off, and I believe John is beginning to notice. I don't like the look in his eyes.

And I heard him ask Jennie a lot of professional questions about me. She had a very good report to give.

She said I slept a good deal in the daytime. John knows I don't sleep very well at night, for all I'm so quiet. He asked me all sorts of questions, too, and pretended to be very loving and kind. As if I couldn't see through him!

Still I don't wonder he acts so, sleeping under this paper for three months.

It only interests me, but I feel sure John and Jennie are secretly affected by it.

+ + + +

Hurrah! This is the last day, but it is enough. John had to stay in town overnight, and won't be out till this evening.

Jennie wanted to sleep with me—the sly thing!—but I told her I should undoubtedly rest better for a night all alone.

That was clever, for really I wasn't alone a bit! As soon as it was moonlight and that poor thing began to crawl and shake the pattern, I got up and ran to help her.

I pulled and she shook, I shook and she pulled, and before morning we had peeled off yards of that paper.

A strip about as high as my head, and half around the room.

And then when the sun came and that awful pattern began to laugh at me I declared I would finish it today!

We go away tomorrow, and they are moving all my furniture down again to leave things as they were before.

Jennie looked at the wall in amazement, but I told her merrily that I did it out of pure spite at the vicious thing.

She laughed and said she wouldn't mind doing it herself, but I must not get tired. How she betrayed herself that time! But I am here, and no person touches this paper but me—not <u>alive</u>!

She tried to get me out of the room—it was too patent! But I said it was so quiet and empty and clean now that I believed I would lie down again and sleep all I could; and not to wake me even for dinner—I would call when I woke!

So now she is gone, and the servants, and the things, and there is nothing left but that great bedstead, nailed down, with the canvas mattress we found on it.

We shall sleep down stairs tonight, and take the boat home tomorrow.

I quite enjoy the room now it is bare again.

She said I slept a good deal in the daytime. 445

John knows I don't sleep very well at night, for all I'm so quiet!

He asked me all sorts of questions, too, and pretended to be very loving and kind.

As if I couldn't see through him!

Still, I don't wonder he acts so, sleeping under this paper for three months. 450

It only interests me, but I feel sure John and Jennie are secretly affected by it.

*   *   *   *   *   *

Hurrah! This is the last day, but it is enough. John is to stay in town over night, and won't be out until this evening.

Jennie wanted to sleep with me—the sly thing! but I told her I should un- 455 doubtedly rest better for a night all alone.

That was clever, for really I wasn't alone a bit! As soon as it was moonlight and that poor thing began to crawl and shake the pattern, I got up and ran to help her.

I pulled and she shook, I shook and she pulled, and before morning we had 460 peeled off yards of that paper.

A strip about as high as my head and half around the room.

And then when the sun came and that awful pattern began to laugh at me, I declared I would finish it to-day!

We go away to-morrow, and they are moving all my furniture down again 465 to leave things as they were before.

Jennie looked at the wall in amazement, but I told her merrily that I did it out of pure spite at the vicious thing.

She laughed and said she wouldn't mind doing it herself, but I must not get tired. 470

How she betrayed herself that time!

But I am here, and no person touches this paper but me,—not *alive!*

She tried to get me out of the room—it was too patent! But I said it was so quiet and empty and clean now that I believed I would lie down again and sleep all I could; and not to wake me even for dinner—I would call when I woke. 475

So now she is gone, and the servants are gone, and the things are gone, and there is nothing left but that great bedstead nailed down, with the canvas mattress we found on it.

We shall sleep downstairs to-night, and take the boat home to-morrow.

I quite enjoy the room, now it is bare again. 480

450   How those children did tear about here! This bedstead is fairly gnawed! But I must get to work.

I have locked the door and thrown the key down into the front path.

I don't want to go out, and I don't want to have anybody come in until John comes. I want to astonish him.

455   I've got a rope up here that even Jennie did not find. If that woman does get out, and tries to get away, I can tie her!

But I forgot I couldn't reach far without anything to stand on! The bed will <u>not</u> move. I tried to lift or push it till I was lame, and then I got so angry I bit off a little piece at one corner—but it hurt my teeth.

460   Then I peeled off all the paper I could reach standing on the floor. It sticks horribly. And the pattern just enjoys it. All those strangled heads and bulbous eyes and waddling fungus growths just shriek with derision!

I am getting angry enough to do something desperate. To jump out of the window would be admirable exercise, but the bars are too strong even to try.

465   Besides, I wouldn't do it of course! I know well enough that a step like that is improper and might be misconstrued.

I don't like to <u>look</u> out of the windows even—there are so many of those creeping women, and they creep so fast.

I wonder if they all came out of that wall paper as I did? But I am securely

470   fastened now by my well-hidden rope—you don't get <u>me</u> out in the road there!

I suppose I shall have to get back behind the pattern when it comes night, and that is hard!

It is so pleasant to be out in this great room and creep around as I please!

I don't want to go outside. I won't, even if Jennie asks me to. For outside

475   you have to creep on the ground, and everything is green instead of yellow.

But here I can creep smoothly on the floor, and my shoulder just fits in that long smooch around the wall, so I can not lose my way.

Why there's John at the door!

It is no use, young man, you can't open it!

480   How he does call and pound!

How those children did tear about here!

This bedstead is fairly gnawed!

But I must get to work.

I have locked the door and thrown the key down into the front path.

I don't want to go out, and I don't want to have anybody come in, till John comes.

I want to astonish him.

I've got a rope up here that even Jennie did not find. If that woman does get out, and tries to get away, I can tie her!

But I forgot I could not reach far without anything to stand on!

This bed will *not* move!

I tried to lift and push it until I was lame, and then I got so angry I bit off a little piece at one corner—but it hurt my teeth.

Then I peeled off all the paper I could reach standing on the floor. It sticks horribly and the pattern just enjoys it! All those strangled heads and bulbous eyes and waddling fungus growths just shriek with derision!

I am getting angry enough to do something desperate. To jump out of the window would be admirable exercise, but the bars are too strong even to try.

Besides I wouldn't do it. Of course not. I know well enough that a step like that is improper and might be misconstrued.

I don't like to *look* out of the windows even—there are so many of those creeping women, and they creep so fast.

I wonder if they all come out of that wall-paper as I did?

But I am securely fastened now by my well-hidden rope—you don't get *me* out in the road there!

I suppose I shall have to get back behind the pattern when it comes night, and that is hard!

It is so pleasant to be out in this great room and creep around as I please!

I don't want to go outside. I won't, even if Jennie asks me to.

For outside you have to creep on the ground, and everything is green instead of yellow.

But here I can creep smoothly on the floor, and my shoulder just fits in that long smooch around the wall, so I cannot lose my way.

Why there's John at the door!

It is no use, young man, you can't open it!

How he does call and pound!

Now he's crying for an ax!

It would be a shame to break that beautiful strong door!

"John dear!" said I in the gentlest voice—"The key is down by the front steps, under a plantain leaf."

485 That silenced him for a few moments.

Then he said—very quietly indeed—"Open the door, my darling!"

"I can't," said I, "The key is down by the front steps under a plantain leaf."

And then I said it again, several times, very gently and slowly.

I said it so often that he had to go and see, and he got it of course, and 490 came in.

He stopped short, by the door. "What is the matter!" he cried. "For God's sake what are you doing!"

I kept on creeping just the same, but I looked at him over my shoulder:

"I've got out at last," said I, "in spite of you and Jane! And I've pulled off most 495 of the paper, so you can't put me back!"

Now why should that man have fainted?

But he did, and right across my path by the wall, so that I had to creep over him!

[signature] *Charlotte Perkins Stetson*

Now he's crying for an axe.

It would be a shame to break down that beautiful door!

"John dear!" said I in the gentlest voice, "the key is down by the front steps, under a plantain leaf!" ₅₂₀

That silenced him for a few moments.

Then he said—very quietly indeed, "Open the door, my darling!"

"I can't," said I. "The key is down by the front door under a plantain leaf!"

And then I said it again, several times, very gently and slowly, and said it so often that he had to go and see, and he got it of course, and came in. He stopped ₅₂₅ short by the door.

"What is the matter?" he cried. "For God's sake, what are you doing!"

I kept on creeping just the same, but I looked at him over my shoulder.

"I've got out at last," said I, "in spite of you and Jane! And I've pulled off most of the paper, so you can't put me back!" ₅₃₀

Now why should that man have fainted? But he did, and right across my path by the wall, so that I had to creep over him every time!

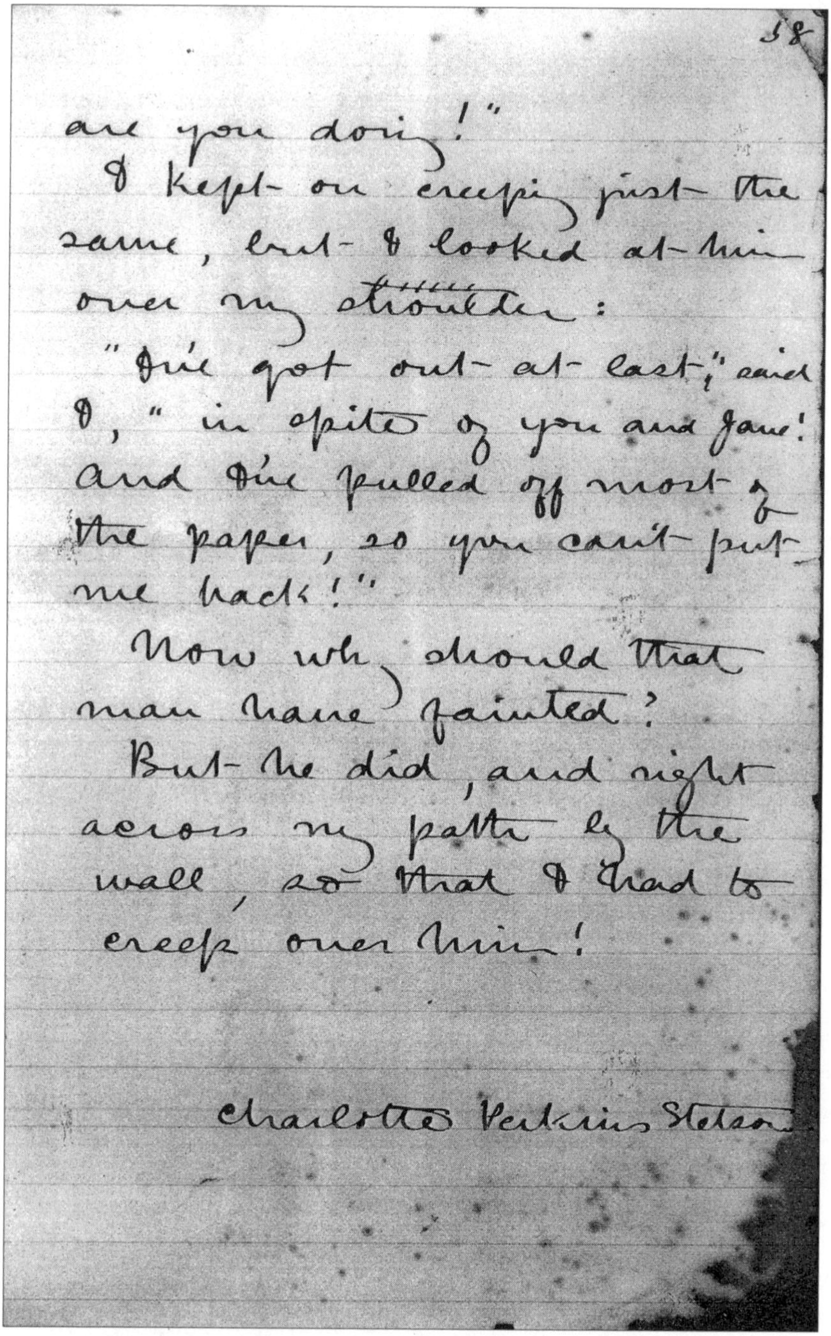

are you doing!"

I kept on creeping just the same, but I looked at him over my shoulder:

"I've got out at last," said I, "in spite of you and Jane! And I've pulled off most of the paper, so you can't put me back!"

Now why should that man have fainted? But he did, and right across my path by the wall, so that I had to creep over him!

Charlotte Perkins Stetson

Figure 1. The final page (p. 58) of Charlotte Perkins Gilman's fair-copy manuscript (MS) of "The Yellow Wall-Paper." *Courtesy of Schlesinger Library on the History of Women in America, Radcliffe Institute, Charlotte Perkins Gilman Papers.*

"I am sitting by the Window in this Atrocious Nursery."

THE YELLOW WALL–PAPER.

By Charlotte Perkins Stetson.

IT is very seldom that mere ordinary people like John and myself secure ancestral halls for the summer.

A colonial mansion, a hereditary estate, I would say a haunted house, and reach the height of romantic felicity—but that would be asking too much of fate!

Still I will proudly declare that there is something queer about it.

Else, why should it be let so cheaply? And why have stood so long untenanted?

John laughs at me, of course, but one expects that in marriage.

John is practical in the extreme. He has no patience with faith, an intense horror of superstition, and he scoffs openly at any talk of things not to be felt and seen and put down in figures.

John is a physician, and *perhaps*— (I would not say it to a living soul, of course, but this is dead paper and a great relief to my mind—) *perhaps* that is one reason I do not get well faster.

You see he does not believe I am sick! And what can one do?

Figure 2. *New England Magazine* text, page 647

I know a little of the principle of design, and I know this thing was not arranged on any laws of radiation, or alternation, or repetition, or symmetry, or anything else that I ever heard of.

It is repeated, of course, by the breadths, but not otherwise.

Looked at in one way each breadth stands alone, the bloated curves and flourishes — a kind of "debased Romanesque" with *delirium tremens* — go waddling up and down in isolated columns of fatuity.

But, on the other hand, they connect diagonally, and the sprawling outlines run off in great slanting waves of optic horror, like a lot of wallowing seaweeds in full chase.

The whole thing goes horizontally, too, at least it seems so, and I exhaust myself in trying' to distinguish the order of its going in that direction.

They have used a horizontal breadth for a frieze, and that adds wonderfully to the confusion.

There is one end of the room where it is almost intact, and there, when the crosslights fade and the low sun shines directly upon it, I can almost fancy radiation after all, — the interminable grotesque seem to form around a common centre and rush off in headlong plunges of equal distraction.

It makes me tired to follow it. I will take a nap I guess.

* * * * * *

I don't know why I should write this.

I don't want to.

I don't feel able.

And I know John' would think it

absurd. But I *must* say what I feel and think in some way — it is such a relief!

But the effort is getting to be greater than the relief.

Half the time now I am awfully lazy, and lie down ever so much.

John says I mustn't lose my strength, and has me take cod liver oil and lots of

"She didn't know I was in the Room."

tonics and things, to say nothing of ale and wine and rare meat.

Dear John ! He loves me very dearly, and hates to have me sick. I tried to have a real earnest reasonable talk with him the other day, and tell him how I wish he would let me go and make a visit to Cousin Henry and Julia.

But he said I wasn't able to go, nor able to stand it after I got there; and I did not make out a very good case for myself, for I was crying before I had finished.

Figure 3. New England Magazine text, page 651

window would be admirable exercise, but the bars are too strong even to try.

Besides I wouldn't do it. Of course not. I know well enough that a step like that is improper and might be miscon-strued.

I don't like to *look* out of the windows even — there are so many of those creep-ing women, and they creep so fast.

I wonder if they all come out of that wall-paper as I did?

But I am securely fastened now by my well-hidden rope — you don't get *me* out in the road there!

I suppose I shall have to get back be-hind the pattern when it comes night, and that is hard!

It is so pleasant to be out in this great room and creep around as I please!

I don't want to go outside. I won't, even if Jennie asks me to.

For outside you have to creep on the ground, and everything is green instead of yellow.

But here I can creep smoothly on the floor, and my shoulder just fits in that long smooch around the wall, so I cannot lose my way.

Why there's John at the door!

It is no use, young man, you can't open it!

How he does call and pound!

Now he's crying for an axe.

It would be a shame to break down that beautiful door!

"John dear!" said I in the gentlest voice, "the key is down by the front steps, under a plaintain leaf!"

That silenced him for a few moments.

Then he said — very quietly indeed, "Open the door, my darling!"

"I can't," said I. "The key is down by the front door under a plantain leaf!"

And then I said it again, several times, very gently and slowly, and said it so often that he had to go and see, and he got it of course, and came in. He stop-ped short by the door.

"What is the matter?" he cried. "For God's sake, what are you doing!"

I kept on creeping just the same, but I looked at him over my shoulder.

"I've got out at last," said I, "in spite of you and Jane? And I've pulled off most of the paper, so you can't put me back!"

Now why should that man have fainted? But he did, and right across my path by the wall, so that I had to creep over him every time!

Figure 4. New England Magazine text, page 656

2. Dueling Interpretations

Speaking a Different Story

THE ILLUSTRATED TEXT

Catherine J. Golden

CHARLOTTE PERKINS GILMAN'S Victorian American tale of a woman undergoing a "rest cure" for nervous depression has given rise to dozens of books, articles, and doctoral dissertations exploring its rich ambiguity. "The Yellow Wall-Paper" is now celebrated in feminist circles and widely anthologized. Nonetheless, many familiar with it are not aware that they have experienced Gilman's landmark short story differently than did the reading public of the late nineteenth century. Nor do they realize that Gilman's work exists in various forms.

The story was first published in the January 1892 issue of the *New England Magazine* with three black-and-white illustrations designed by a staff illustrator named Jo. H. Hatfield. Small, Maynard of Boston reprinted the story (unillustrated) in 1899 as a fifty-five-page chapbook; the boards, which contain a sulfur yellow pattern on a dark-orange background, resemble wallpaper and bring to bear the dominant motif of the story, whose pattern at first repels but then fascinates the nameless narrator required to rest in her nursery-prison. First anthologized in William Dean Howells's *The Great Modern American Stories: An Anthology* (1920), the 1892 text without illustrations is typically recognized as the authoritative text.[1] Gilman's handwritten manuscript in the Gilman Papers at the Schlesinger Library (ca. 1890–91) has not had premier authority, although the prioritizing of a manuscript version is often a guiding principle in textual criticism of nineteenth-century American authors, as Fredson Bowers argues.[2] The republication history of "The Yellow Wall-Paper" follows, rather, the recommendation of another leading textual authority, Philip Gaskell: the first printed edition, and not the fair copy, should be preferred ("the actual writing of the manuscript . . . is a means of composition, not an end").[3] First reprinted in 1994 in Denise D. Knight's *"The Yellow Wall-Paper" and Selected Stories of Charlotte Perkins Gilman,* the manuscript—republished in this edition—is also grounded in the author's intentions. If we accept the impossibility of a single "authoritative" text of "The Yellow Wall-Paper," a controversial point in textual studies that this edition raises, then we must also recognize significant differences between what might be considered competing texts of a work.

Critics tend to privilege a purely linguistic text over the material condition in which that text appears in a book or magazine. Sadly, many Victorian novels created through and with pictorial capitals and full-page or marginal let-in illustrations are reprinted today with few or no images at all. Counter to the trend in anthologizing "The Yellow Wall-Paper," my interest lies in the condition in which the 1892 text appeared in the *New England Magazine.* That text contains what Jerome McGann calls "bibliographical codes"—a pictorial capital, rows of asterisks between sections of the story, and three illustrations—that interact with the language of the text, offering a different way of reading the story.[4] Investigating the nature of textuality, McGann argues that a text is "a laced network of linguistic and bibliographical codes."[5] He defines bibliographical codes as those textual features not regularly studied: ink, typeface, page format, bindings, paper, and so forth. Calling attention to the authority of the editor over an "original work," McGann elsewhere states, "If we think of the literary work as a physical object, as a book with particular sorts of content that come first to the attention of our eyes and then of our minds, we may begin to see what a peculiar version of the 'original work' is being presented to us in critical editions."[6] McGann's claim has bearing on the various editions of "The Yellow Wall-Paper" that reprint the story as an independent book or part of a collection. Moreover, in the 1892 *New England Magazine* text, bibliographical features commonly used in turn-of-the-century periodicals come readily to the "attention of our eyes" and bias our interpretation of the story.

When preparing a casebook on "The Yellow Wall-Paper" in the early 1990s, I accidentally discovered the illustrations. I had sought out the story in the *New England Magazine* to determine whether it first appeared in January 1892 or May 1892, as critics variously noted. To compound the confusion, Gilman suggests in her autobiography that the publication date is May 1891.[7] I confirmed the publi-

Gilman projects mental derangement onto a familiar literary figure, a middle-class wife and mother. She places the source of madness in the sacrosanct sphere for dutiful women—the home—leading some contemporary reviewers to urge that the story be kept away from impressionable young women. Even William Dean Howells, in his introduction to *The Great Modern American Stories,* notes, "It wanted at least two generations to freeze our young blood with Mrs. Perkins Gilman's story of *The Yellow Wall Paper.* . . . Now that I have got it into my collection here, I shiver over it as much as I did when I read it in manuscript, though I agree with the editor of *The Atlantic* of the time that it was too terribly good to be printed."[12] In showing a marked deterioration of the narrator's mental state, the illustrations intensify the Poesque line of response and correspond to commonly held beliefs of madness in late nineteenth-century Britain and America. Female gender, heredity, and overindulgence in reading and writing were thought to predispose an individual to madness.[13] Gilman's nameless female narrator, who very much wants to write, is pictured doing so against her doctor's orders.

Very little information exists on the illustrator, Jo. H. Hatfield, a regular illustrator for the *New England Magazine.* That monthly Boston publication, which absorbed the *Bay State Monthly,* ran from 1886 to 1900. The magazine was "devoted to the History, Biography, Literature, Education and General Interests of the New England States and People." Hatfield illustrated fiction and nonfiction principally between 1891 and 1893, working independently, as in the case of "The Yellow Wall-Paper," and in collaboration with other illustrators, commonly H. Martin Beal and Louis A. Holman. For example, Hatfield is sole illustrator of three stories in the *New England Magazine:* "Dr. Cabot's Two Brains" by Jeannette B. Perry, "The Governor's Reception" by Frances M. Abbott, and "The Squire's Niece Maria" by Mary F. Haynes. For "Annals of an Ancient Parish," an essay by Rev. William H. Savage, Hatfield is one of eight illustrators. And, along with Beale, Hatfield illustrated Lee C. Harby's "In the Old South State."[14] The artist signed the three illustrations accompanying "The Yellow Wall-Paper" as Jo. H. Hatfield, though the signature appears variously in the *New England Magazine* as J. H. Hatfield, J H Hatfield, J H. Hatfield, and Jo. H. H. Further investigation reveals the illustrator is Joseph Henry Hatfield (1863–1928), a Canadian-born turn-of-the-century Boston painter known for genre and landscape paintings as well as for being a careful observer of childhood.[15] Dates, location, and signature confirm the match. In John Castagno's *American Artists* (1990), Joseph Henry Hatfield's signature appears as J H Hatfield, one of the variations in the *New England Magazine* illustrations. Moreover, the signature in Castagno's book and all variations in the magazine illustrations show a single line crossing the two *H*s, a distinguishing mark.[16]

Born near Kingston, Ontario, Joseph Henry Hatfield studied in the Parisian ateliers under Jean-Joseph Benjamin-Constant, Lucien Doucet, and Jules Lefebrve in 1889 and 1890. Moving to the Boston area, he won a silver medal from the Massachusetts Charitable Mechanics Association in 1892 and exhibited and won second prize at the National Academy of Design in 1896. He also exhibited at the Paris Salon in 1891 and at the Boston Art Club from 1888 to 1902.[17] It is not surprising that Hatfield freelanced for a magazine. In the nineteenth century, the lucrative field of book and magazine illustration lured leading painters on both sides of the Atlantic to dabble in illustration—Sir John Everett Millais is a prime example. Other artists, notably Winslow Homer, launched artistic careers through illustration.

Hatfield's illustrations for the *New England Magazine* demonstrate his talents for genre and landscape painting. The illustrations for "The Yellow Wall-Paper" and "The Squire's Niece Maria" show figures in domestic interior scenes common in genre painting. In one of the illustrations for "The Governor's Reception," which bears the caption "Don't seem to be any signs of breakin' the drouth" (305), Hatfield places two well-drawn farmworkers, a man and a youth, in a field surrounded by haystacks, revealing his talent for delineating figure and landscape. Another skillfully executed drawing, this one in the story "In the Old South State," shows a grand Southern home and bears the caption "The House in which Lafayette first slept in America." This drawing looks more like a painting than a magazine illustration. Hatfield includes rich shading and careful architectural details—columns, an open porch, window treatments, and an upper balcony—as well as trees and shrubs all around.

Gilman makes no mention of Hatfield's illustrations in her diary, autobiography, or letters. Such an omission might seem puzzling, since Gilman was herself an artist. Several of her stories published around the time of "The Yellow Wall-Paper," such as "The Giant Wistaria" (1891) and "The Lake of Mrs. Johnsmith" (1898), also appear with illustrations.[18] But none of Gilman's fiction in the *Forerunner*—the liberal journal she single-handedly wrote, edited, and published for just over seven years (1909–16)—is illustrated. Gilman elects not to mention the illustrations to "The Yellow Wall-Paper," although she refers to the story at length in her autobiography, *The Living of Charlotte Perkins Gilman,* and her 1913 *Forerunner* article "Why I Wrote 'The Yellow Wallpaper'?" Authorial silence suggests these elements of the 1892 version lay beyond the author's control.[19] No doubt owing to the customs of magazine and book publishing of the time, the *New England Magazine* text and the 1899 Small, Maynard chapbook with its colorful patterned boards are collaborative productions of author, illustrator, and publisher.

The bibliographical features of "The Yellow Wall-Paper" appear consistently throughout the magazine. Feature articles and essays begin with illustrated pictorial capitals. The pictorial capital *I* that launches Gilman's landmark story seems ornamental, rather than illustrative of theme or plot (see fig. 2). Two triangles form a large square, which surrounds most of the letter *I*. The bottom triangle is blank, but the top one contains a design that could be read as the wallpaper pattern that mesmerizes the narrator to the puzzlement of Jennie and John. A decorative vine motif forms an S curve arching around the *I*, while another vine climbs to the top of the letter. Again, a reader could conceivably interpret this motif as an indication of the undulating patterns of the ubiquitous wallpaper. However, Hatfield uses floral-vine imagery in combination with this same pattern of a square composed of two triangles (in some instances encasing the entire letter) in his pictorial capitals for other stories, such as Perry's "Dr. Cabot's Two Brains" and Haynes's "The Squire's Niece Maria." The pictorial capital that introduces "The Yellow Wall-Paper" does not foreshadow material to come in the manner of, for example, William Thackeray's midcentury pictorial capitals for *Vanity Fair* (1848), which presage Becky Sharp's husband hunting and advance the siren motif.[20]

The use of asterisks in "The Yellow Wall-Paper" shows how a seemingly minor bibliographical code informs our reading of the story. A first-person narrative, "The Yellow Wall-Paper" unfolds as a diary that the narrator keeps. Her husband, John, a physician of high standing, forbids her to write. Stopping when John or her sister-in-law Jennie approaches, the narrator nonetheless writes in secret. The twelve entries, which constitute the entire linguistic text, record the narrator's impressions of her summer stay in an ancestral hall in the country.[21] The entries, which get shorter as the story proceeds, also reveal incremental changes in the narrator's mental state.

The entries are undated and separated in the fair-copy manuscript by four asterisks, each set flush with the left-hand margin. In the *New England Magazine*, which prints two columns of text on each page, these asterisks become more aesthetically pleasing. Six asterisks form a row, centered in the column of text, which forms half of the page. The shift in the aspect of the asterisks, though seemingly minor, makes clearer the delineations between entries and thus clarifies Gilman's intention that the story itself be read as a secret diary. On the other hand, the dual columns of text diminish the sensation that an entry has ended, since the asterisks are centered only in one of the two columns, yet the eye perceives both columns when reading each page. Howells's 1920 reprinting of the 1892 magazine text keeps the asterisks and improves them. The number of asterisks increases to eight; the line of asterisks is centered, extending nearly across the entire page of text. In contrast, the 1973 Feminist Press edition, which directed a great deal of attention to the story, reprints the 1892 text without the illustrations or the asterisks, leaving several lines of blank space between entries. As a result, the 1973 edition gives the impression that there are only ten entries, since in two cases a page break coincides with the end of a diary entry. The 1996 revised Feminist Press edition importantly reinstates the centered rows of six asterisks (though not the columns) as used in the *New England Magazine.* The 2004 Routledge sourcebook on "The Yellow Wall-Paper," which I edited, also retains the centered rows of asterisks.

I cite this publication history to illustrate two points: different textual versions of the work seemingly compete, and a bibliographical feature as seemingly insignificant as an asterisk can make a difference in reading a linguistic text. If the narrator-diarist is writing for an imagined self, the way she imagines that self clearly changes as the diary entries progress. For example, the narrator weakly refers to herself as "one" in the opening entry and "myself" in the opening sentence of the *New England Magazine* text—as opposed to "I" in the opening sentence of the manuscript. Growing bolder, she increasingly authors sentences using "I," beginning with the fourth entry. Rows of asterisks, as presented in the *New England Magazine,* clearly indicate where each entry begins and ends, allowing the reader to mark changes in the narrator's state of mind and self-expression.

The three illustrations correspond to specific lines of the story. The caption "I am sitting by the Window in this Atrocious Nursery" paraphrases a line from the second entry of the story that reads, "I am sitting by the window now, up in this atrocious nursery, and there is nothing to hinder my writing as much as I please, save lack of strength" (*NEM,* 89–90).[22] The illustration is prominently positioned as a headpiece to the entire story as well as the first diary entry, not the second entry, to which it refers. In contrast to nineteenth-century authors she admired—with Charles Dickens a prime example—Gilman offers no linguistic indication of the narrator's appearance. Hatfield draws a respectable-looking Victorian woman, sitting in a rocking chair by the window. Her hair is neatly swept into a bun. Her conventional dress, with high collar and long fitted sleeves, makes her look demure. Her expression seems "practical in the extreme" (*NEM,* 9), much as she describes John in the opening entry. However, Hatfield captures her writing, an act that directly defies the patriarchal forces administering her "rest cure": the narrator's physician-husband John—"There comes John, and I must put this away,—he hates to have me write a word" (*NEM,* 84–85); her brother, "also a physician, and also of high standing, and he says the same thing" (*NEM,* 20–21); S. Weir Mitchell, the foremost specialist in women's nervous diseases, whom Gilman indicts in the story (*NEM,* 185–87); and her sister-in-law Jennie, "a perfect and enthusiastic housekeeper" (*NEM*, 166), who "thinks it is the writing which made me sick!" (*NEM*, 167). Hatfield includes the bars on the windows of the former nursery, an embodiment of the restrictions of her gendered world.

The narrator tells us of her covert action in her first diary entry: "congenial work, with excitement and change, would do me good" (*NEM*, 26–27); she also confesses, "I did write for a while in spite of them" (*NEM*, 29). In the illustration, she holds the pen and diary—presumably the diary we are reading. The inkwell by her side facilitates the act of writing. Her gaze is wholly unselfconscious. Her lowered eyes turn to the pages she is writing—and we are reading—suggesting her active engagement in her own secret diary.

The second illustration (see fig. 3) is not as well executed as the first and third, which mark the narrator's progression from sanity to madness. The caption takes a line from the sixth diary entry, "She didn't know I was in the room" (*NEM*, 346), but the marginal let-in illustration is positioned midway through the story in the third entry. Of interest, Hatfield lightly indicates the flamboyant undulating pattern of the paper only in the section framing Jennie. The narrator wears the same dress as in the previous illustration, and her hairstyle again is a respectable bun. But the narrator's expression, which now looks clouded, arguably conveys the beginnings of her hallucinatory state, well established by this point in the story where the narrator sees the figure of a woman "stooping down and creeping about behind that pattern" (*NEM*, 259–60).

The illustration initiates the narrator's mounting paranoia and establishes the antagonism between the narrator and Jennie even earlier than the linguistic text. This image realizes the narrator's suspiciousness of Jennie, who has an "inexplicable look" (*NEM*, 340) as she gazes at the narrator while keeping her left hand on the wallpaper. The narrator fears Jennie is "studying that pattern, and I am determined that nobody shall find it out but myself!" (*NEM*, 353–54). The narrator stops writing in her diary when she realizes "There's sister on the stairs!" (*NEM*, 178). Thus, she responds the same way to Jennie as to John: "There comes John, and I must put this away,—he hates to have me write a word" (*NEM*, 84–85). Jennie's allegiance lies with her brother John, "a physician of high standing" (*NEM*, 17). Like John, Jennie "is practical in the extreme" (*NEM*, 9). Jennie arguably acts as the narrator's jailer. Although the two women dress alike, no bond exists between them, a theme we find in much of Gilman's later fiction.[23] Jennie is part of the patriarchy that restricts the narrator and against which she rebels.

Hatfield positions the third and final illustration as a dramatic tailpiece to the story (see fig. 4). There is no caption. We see the narrator crawling over her unconscious husband directly below the final lines of the story that it illustrates: "Now why should that man have fainted? But he did, and right across my path by the wall, so that I had to creep over him every time!" (*NEM,* 531–32). At a time when clothing and coiffure marked one's age, class, gender, and temperament, the narrator's altered hairstyle alone speaks volumes to the Victorian audience of the *New England Magazine.* While her neat bun in the first image expresses her respectability, her wild hair in the third plate signals her insanity. The narrator's long and frizzled mane drapes down her back, over her shoulder, and on top of John, who lies beneath her in a dead faint. She seems detached from the torn bits of wallpaper on the floor next to her and John, which could be read as a literal representation of the source of her insanity. Just as Gilman does not describe the narrator in the opening entries, nothing in the text even hints at a change in the narrator's appearance. In his final dramatic illustration, Hatfield visually projects onto Gilman's text the Victorian conception of the long- and wild-haired madwoman of literature, *Jane Eyre's* Bertha Mason par excellence.

This visual projection, no doubt responding to the narrator's hallucinations and action of tearing off the wallpaper to free the woman trapped behind its pattern, condemn her to madness. The finale of the text, in turn, reinforces this illustration. The words "every time" in the closing line of the 1892 text suggest that the narrator's circling the perimeter of the room remains ongoing. In the manuscript version, the final line of the story reads, "so that I had to creep over him!" (MS, 497–98). To Victorian readers, the addition of the adverbial phrase "every time" accentuates the insanity of her actions, convincingly rendered in the illustration. John's defenselessness and the narrator's self-absorption, as well as her crazed and disheveled look, no doubt encouraged one of the original readings of the story: a Poesque horror tale. The striking transformation in the narrator's appearance conveys the alarming rate at which she passes from "slight mental derangement to raving lunacy," to quote one anonymous 1892 reviewer in the *Boston Evening Transcript.*[24] Even today, some of my Skidmore College students who "read" the illustrations attribute defeat and madness, not triumph, to the narrator. "She clearly looks insane . . . her madness has fully developed," to quote a typical student response.

Early twenty-first-century readers often interpret the narrator's final state and change in coiffure differently. Her hair, now freed from its confining style, can be read as a symbol of personal liberation from the restrictions of patriarchy.[25] The narrator, creeping over John, conveys a shift in gender roles. Her right hand, positioned at a sharp angle, suggests she is pressing John's face into the floor as she crawls over him. Her eyes show no recognition that "that man" (*NEM,* 531) is John—the husband to whom she initially defers and refers to by name even though she calls herself "one" and "myself." Temporarily defeated, swooning John assumes a fetal position, accentuating his vulnerability. In contrast, the narrator, who increasingly authors sentences with "I," indicates a more forceful sense of self, as when she exclaims, "'I've got out at last,' said I" (*NEM*, 529). In her final depiction, the narrator, in some readers' eyes, triumphs over patriarchy and John's prescription for sanity, or she achieves at least a dubious victory, as I have elsewhere argued.[26]

Critics have read "The Yellow Wall-Paper" from a range of perspectives: feminist, linguistic, psychoanalytical, sociological, new historicist, biographical, and a combination of the above. Rarely have the bibliographical codes accompanying the story been a gloss to read the text. I have argued here that we should not privilege only the linguistic text of "The Yellow Wall-Paper": the appearance of the story matters. The rows of asterisks between diary entries and the three illustrations function as bibliographical codes that produce meaning in the 1892 magazine version. In comparison to the three other texts I have discussed—Gilman's manuscript; the 1899 Small, Maynard chapbook; or the 1892 version reprinted without bibliographical features—the 1892 illustrated text as it appeared in the *New England Magazine* speaks a different story.

Notes

1. William Dean Howells, ed., *The Great Modern American Stories* (New York: Boni and Liveright, 1920). For a listing of reprintings of "The Yellow Wall-Paper," see entry 505 in Gary Scharnhorst, *Charlotte Perkins Gilman: A Bibliography* (Metuchen, NJ: Scarecrow Press, 1985), 60; Julie Bates Dock, *"The Yellow Wall-paper" and the History of Its Publication and Reception* (University Park: Pennsylvania State University Press, 1998), app., 121–32. I also include a partial list of reprintings in my chronology in *Charlotte Perkins Gilman's "The Yellow Wall-Paper": A Sourcebook and Critical Edition,* ed. Catherine J. Golden (London: Routledge, 2004), 17–25.

2. See Jerome McGann, introduction to *A Critique of Modern Textual Criticism* (Chicago: University of Chicago Press, 1983), 5–6. For more detailed information, see Fredson Bowers, "Some Principles for Scholarly Editions of Nineteenth-Century American Authors," *Studies in Bibliography* 17 (1964): 223–28.

3. Philip Gaskell, *A New Introduction to Bibliography* (Oxford: Oxford University Press, 1972), 340.

4. For information on bibliographical codes, see Jerome McGann, *The Textual Condition* (Princeton, NJ: Princeton University Press, 1991), 13. I preserve these codes in my 2004 Routledge sourcebook and use footnotes to indicate differences between the manuscript and 1892 versions.

5. McGann, *Textual Condition*, 13.

6. McGann, *Critique*, 90.

7. The story first appeared in the *New England Magazine* 5 (January 1892): 647–56 under the name of Charlotte Perkins Stetson. The confusion surrounding the date likely stems from con-

ventions for binding journals at the turn of the twentieth century. Volume 5 contains six numbers, September 1891 through February 1892. If *NEM* bound issues by year of publication, as we do today, volume 11, number 5 would have been May, not January, 1892. The entire run of the *New England Magazine* is available online.

In *The Living of Charlotte Perkins Gilman: An Autobiography* (New York: D. Appleton-Century Co., 1935; repr., New York: Arno Press, 1972; Harper and Row, 1975), Gilman reprints a letter written to the *New England Magazine* that suggests the publication date was May 1891 (p. 119). Gilman has other inaccuracies in her autobiography (e.g., listing Howells's collection as *Masterpieces in American Fiction,* rather than *Great Modern American Stories* [65]).

8. Charlotte Perkins Stetson to Martha Luther Lane, July 27, 1890, Rhode Island Historical Society, quoted in Gary Scharnhorst's biography, *Charlotte Perkins Gilman* (Boston: Twayne, 1985), 17. The letter also appears in my 2004 Routledge sourcebook on "The Yellow Wall-Paper," 26–27. Gustave Doré was one of the most prominent and successful French book illustrators of the mid–nineteenth century. He gained acclaim for his illustrations to books including Dante's *Inferno* (1861), *Don Quixote* (1862), and the Bible (1866). Both Poe and Doré's work is characterized by a very spirited love of the grotesque and the bizarre. I believe Gilman's written text (*not* any illustrations) is being compared to Doré's work as well as Poe's: in the nineteenth century, it was common for an author to have artistic role models. Dickens was heavily influenced by Hogarth, for example.

9. In her helpful section "Reviews" (102–19) in *"The Yellow Wall-paper" and the History of Its Publication and Reception,* Dock reprints Blackwell's review and identifies his importance. For a typical piece focusing on the wallpaper, see the anonymous 1899 review identified as being from the *Baltimore Times,* 106.

10. Scharnhorst, *Twayne,* 17.

11. See Denise D. Knight, ed. *The Diaries of Charlotte Perkins Gilman* (Charlottesville: University Press of Virginia, 1994). For example, in an entry dated Thursday, January 8, 1885, Gilman reports exchanging "Jennie's Keats for two books of Poe's tales" (310). In another entry dated Monday, March 21, 1887, Gilman notes, "Sam lends me one of Poe's works" (380).

12. Howells, *The Great Modern American Stories,* vii.

13. For example, Dr. Edward H. Clarke, a retired professor from the Harvard Medical School, argued that girls who studied during menstruation and throughout the process of sexual development diverted essential energy from their reproductive organs. Subsequently, they suffered from a host of ailments including menorrhagia, dysmenorrhea, hemorrhage, amenorrhea, headache, dyspepsia, invalidism, neuralgia, hysteria, intense insanity, and death. Clarke, *Sex in Education; Or, A Fair Chance for the Girls* (1873; repr., New York: Arno Press, 1972).

14. Perry, *NEM* 11 (November 1891): 344–54; Abbott, *NEM* 12 (May 1892): 301–11; Haynes, *NEM* 12 (June 1892): 461–72; Savage, *NEM* 12 (April 1892): 237–56; Harby, *NEM* 13 (January 1893): 670–75.

15. See Sadakichi Hartmann, *A History of American Art,* 2 vols. (New York: Tudor, 1934), 2:122.

16. See John Castagno, *American Artists: Signatures and Monograms, 1800–1989* (Metuchen, NJ: Scarecrow Press, 1990), 304.

17. See, for example, Mantle Fielding, *Mantle Fielding's Dictionary of American Painters, Sculptors and Engravers,* ed. Glenn B. Opitz, 2d ed. (Poughkeepsie, NY: Apollo, 1986), 384; Peter Hastings Falk, editor in chief, *Who Was Who in American Art, 1564–1975,* 3 vols. (Madison, CT: Sound View Press, 1999), 2:1491. See also Golden's "'The Yellow Wall-Paper' and Joseph Henry Hatfield's Original Magazine Illustrations," *ANQ* 18 (Spring 2005): 53–63.

18. Some of the signatures of the illustrators are difficult to decipher. For example, "The Giant Wistaria" appeared with two illustrations by two different artists, G. Satig(?) and Stacy Tolman, in *NEM*, n.s., 4 (June 1891): 480–85; "The Lake of Mrs. Johnsmith" appeared with three illustrations by G. H. Underwood in *Criterion* 18 (October 22, 1898): 3–4; and "Mrs. Beazley's Deeds" first appeared, with three illustrations by Pobein(?), in *Woman's World* 27 (March 1911): 12–13, 58.

19. Two chapters in *Living* bear scrutiny. In "The Breakdown," Gilman describes how she undergoes Mitchell's "Rest Cure" treatment, which she indicts in this story. In "Pasadena," she divulges her personal motivation for writing the story of a woman's breakdown. She explains both the autobiographical roots and her intentions for writing the story in "Why I Wrote 'The Yellow Wallpaper'?" *Forerunner* 4 (October 1913): 271.

20. See, for example, the pictorial capital for chapter 4, which depicts Becky fishing, in the very chapter in which Becky attempts to hook Amelia Sedley's rich brother, Joseph Sedley, into marriage.

21. For a linguistic reading of the twelve diarylike entries, see "The Writing of 'The Yellow Wallpaper': A Double Palimpsest," in *The Captive Imagination: A Casebook on 'The Yellow Wallpaper,'* ed. Catherine Golden (New York: Feminist Press, 1992), 296–306; repr. in Denise D. Knight, *Charlotte Perkins Gilman: A Study of the Short Fiction* (New York: Twayne, 1997), 155–65. For an approach to teaching the language of the story, see Golden, "Teaching 'The Yellow Wall-Paper' through the Lens of Language," in *Approaches to Teaching Gilman's "The Yellow Wall-Paper" and "Herland,"* ed. Denise D. Knight and Cynthia J. Davis (New York: Modern Language Association of America, 2003), 53–60.

22. Parenthetical references to *NEM* refer to line numbers of the critical text printed in this edition.

23. The "older, wiser woman," a term Gilman herself uses in her short story "Turned" (1911) to describe Marion Marroner, also speaks to a type of character in Gilman's oeuvre who rises to the aid of her younger sister-woman to seek "a common good." Works that exhibit bonding between women include "Turned" (*Forerunner*, September 1911), "Making a Change" (*Forerunner*, December 1911), "His Mother" (*Forerunner*, July 1914), "The Girl in the Pink Hat" (*Forerunner*, February 1916), and *Unpunished* (ca. 1929, ed. Catherine J. Golden and Denise D. Knight [New York: Feminist Press, 1997]).

24. See M. D., "PERILOUS STUFF," *Boston Evening Transcript*, April 8, 1892, p. 6, col. 2. This review is reprinted in the 2004 Routledge sourcebook on "The Yellow Wall-Paper," 81–82.

25. Loose hair in the Victorian period is also associated with sexual liberation and impropriety, as holds true in the characterization of Bertha Mason. However, the changes in the narrator's appearance arguably speak today of gaining personal, not sexual, freedom.

26. See Golden, "The Writing of 'The Yellow Wallpaper'" (Twayne), 155–65, or entry 12 in the 2004 Routledge sourcebook, 153–54.

"I am getting angry enough to do something desperate"

THE QUESTION OF FEMALE "MADNESS"

Denise D. Knight

CRITICS OF "The Yellow Wall-Paper" have long argued that the confessional narrator of Gilman's most famous work is "insane" at the end of the story. As early as 1892, a review in the *Boston Evening Transcript* referred to the "raving lunacy" of the narrator.[1] When the chapbook edition was published by Small, Maynard & Company in 1899, several reviewers characterized the narrator as insane.[2] Contemporary critics, too, have continued to identify insanity as the condition that plagues the protagonist of the story. In 1973, when the popular Feminist Press edition of "The Yellow Wall-Paper" was first published, Elaine Hedges declared that the defeated narrator had failed "to retain her sanity."[3] Other critics were quick to concur with Hedges's opinion, though readings have varied as to whether the narrator's "insanity" is a form of triumph or defeat.[4] While such interpretations have been widely accepted and invite a host of theoretical readings from feminist criticism to psychoanalytical examinations of the narrator and text, they ignore subtle indications that the narrator's behavior at the end of the story may not be a form of insanity but rather a deliberate act of rebellion—an expression of the tremendous rage she feels toward her husband, John.

This alternative reading is based on three crucial pieces of evidence. First, the story's narrator is apparently capable of articulating both rational thought and moral judgment during the events leading up to and including John's fainting spell, a point that has been addressed directly by only one critic, Richard Feldstein.[5] Second, the 1892 *New England Magazine* printing of "The Yellow Wall-Paper"— the version most commonly anthologized—adds some ninety paragraph breaks to the story, causing the narrative to be considerably more fragmented than Gilman's handwritten manuscript (the preferred text for this analysis).[6] As a result, the narrator's disjointed thought pattern is both distorted and exaggerated in the *New England Magazine* edition. Moreover, an analysis of the manuscript version, when compared to the 1892 *New England Magazine* version, reveals variants that subtly underscore the simmering anger experienced by the narrator. Finally, in three different discussions of the story, Gilman quotes a physician, Dr. Brummell Jones, who described "The Yellow Wall-Paper" as "the best study of *incipient* insanity" (emphasis added) he had ever seen,[7] a characterization Gilman did not dispute. This point is noteworthy since the adjective *incipient* suggests merely the preliminary stages of insanity, rather than a full descent into "madness," as the majority of critics have insisted.[8] Indeed, critics have long argued that because the story's narrator has been forbidden by her husband to write, she turns her attentions to a substitute text—the wallpaper—which quickly becomes the object of her obsession. The critics point to the infantile regression apparently exhibited by the narrator at the story's end, when she creeps around the room on her hands and knees, as evidence that she has lost her mind.

However, Feldstein argues that if we allow an ironic interpretation of "The Yellow Wall-Paper," the narrator's "'regression' becomes purposeful—a cunning craziness, a militant, politicized madness by which the narrator resists the interiorization of authority" imposed by John and her brother, both of whom are physicians. Feldstein further contends that "once [the narrator] understands this patriarchal logic," which refuses to consider her own intuitive ideas about her treatment, she "rechannels her effort into the symbolic sphere to counter John's simplistic notion of . . . reality" and finds "another effective means to register her dissatisfaction with the inequity of their relationship."[9] Feldstein maintains that the protagonist "*chooses* to act out," in effect, altering John's view of her condition through actions since he remains unresponsive to her words. It is an ingenious interpretation made more compelling by two facts: the narrator's tremendous resentment at being "forbidden to 'work'" (MS, 20),[10] and the resulting anger that she experiences throughout the text.[11]

From the first page of the story, the issue of "work" is a source of contention between the narrator and her husband, as is his contempt of her fanciful imagination. The narrator, apparently a writer, confides that John has declared her activity off-limits until she is "well again" (MS, 21), though she personally believes "that congenial work with excitement and change" would do her good (MS, 23). Since her husband is a physician, however, a fact about which he takes every opportunity to remind her, she initially acquiesces to his prescription to rest. Still, she believes in the therapeutic benefits of writing: "I think sometimes that if I were only well enough to write a little it would relieve the pressure of ideas and rest me" (MS, 122–23). Worse yet, however, is the lack of "advice and companionship about [her] work" (MS, 125), a condition that undoubtedly evokes frustration and anger, particularly since she disagrees with John's ideas. In fact, after lamenting the lack of companionship, she admits for the first time how angry she gets, although she deflects the anger onto the wallpaper, rather than directing it at John: "I get positively angry with the impertinence of it [the wallpaper], and the everlastingness" (MS, 132). If, however, the wallpaper pattern signifies the symbolic suffocation of women in an oppressive patriarchal society, as suggested by the images of "strangled heads and bulbous eyes" (MS, 461–62), then we can view the deflection as a form of subterfuge, since proper Victorian women were discouraged from displaying anger. But, as Elizabeth Ammons suggests, by the end of the story, the wallpaper's "exterior 'surface' violence transforms into what it has been in part all along: the external manifestation of the narrator's internalized rage."[12] The narrator has previously acknowledged the progressive escalation in her anger when she confides, "I am getting angry enough to do something desperate" (MS, 463). Although "jump[ing] out of the window would be admirable exercise," she "know[s] well enough that a step like that is improper and might be misconstrued" (MS, 463–66). Still, she is "desperate" and "angry" enough to do something that will convince John of the seriousness of her condition. As Ammons remarks, the narrator is so incensed by her condition that "she moves from the position of victim to that of agent."[13] In effect, by destroying the wallpaper and crawling around the room, the narrator refutes John's brash denial of her illness by demonstrating that she will, indeed, be "as sick as she pleases" (MS, 274–75), since that is the only way she can convince him of the gravity of her case.

The narrator, in fact, is not unlike the character of Sarah Penn in Mary E. Wilkins Freeman's story, "The Revolt of 'Mother.'"[14] Sarah's pleas to her husband to build her a new house—a promise he had made some forty years earlier— continually fall on deaf ears, and like John, Adoniram Penn refuses to discuss his wife's concerns. He tells her he "can't stan' here talkin' all day" and that he "ain't got nothin' to say" (302), statements reminiscent of John's rebuke in "Wall-Paper" when his wife attempts to discuss her condition with him late one night. John dismisses her concerns and promises to "talk about it in the morning," a pledge he apparently fails to keep (MS, 275–76). Tired of living in her little "box of a house" (297), which forms a parallel to the narrator's isolation in a wallpapered attic, Freeman's

Sarah rebels while Adoniram is out of town by moving their household (furniture, children, and all) into the spacious newly built barn and converting it into a home. Freeman writes that Sarah's behavior seems so dramatically out of character that "some held her to be *insane;* some, of a lawless and rebellious spirit" (309, emphasis added). Like Gilman's narrator, Sarah is perceived by some to have gone insane, since her actions are dramatically out of character for the usually meek housewife and mother. Yet, as Marjorie Pryse contends, it is Sarah's rebellion that finally empowers her: "Sarah's 'revolt' ends her subordination because she manages through her actions what she could never accomplish with words: she alters [her husband's] view of her condition" (326). The same can be said of the narrator in "The Yellow Wall-Paper." Because John refuses to listen to his wife, who "personally disagrees" with his ideas about her treatment, she can finally only modify his perception of her circumstances by forcing him to *see* what he has refused to hear. It is a combination of rage and rebellion that drives her to such drastic ends. So powerful is the visual depiction of her condition—a condition John refuses to acknowledge—that he faints when he finally gains entrance to the locked room.

Similarly, in Kate Chopin's 1899 novel *The Awakening,* Edna Pontellier's husband, Léonce, begins "to wonder if his wife were not growing a little unbalanced mentally"[15] after she begins to reject her socially prescribed roles and to assert her independence, in part by indulging her desire to paint. Léonce Pontellier had grown accustomed to "a certain tacit submissiveness in his wife. But her new and unexpected line of conduct completely bewildered him. It shocked him. Then her absolute disregard for her duties as a wife angered him" (61). Edna, however, grows angry too, smashing a crystal vase and stamping on her wedding ring (56–57). By the end of the novel, her resentment toward her prescribed roles is apparent: "The children appeared before her like antagonists who had overcome her; who had overpowered and sought to drag her into the soul's slavery for the rest of her days" (123). Although "Léonce and the children . . . were a part of her life . . . they need not have thought they could possess her body and soul" (124). Like Sarah and the narrator of "Wall-Paper," Edna Pontellier alters her husband's view of her condition in the final scene. She sheds her clothing, walks into the ocean, and drowns. Her disrobing is the ultimate act of rebellion: the "proper" Victorian woman, naked in death, ensures that she has the last word. In the event that her nude body is eventually recovered, it will provide proof positive that hers was no accidental drowning. On the contrary, while some would hold her to be insane, like Gilman's narrator, Edna has made a defiant and deliberate statement through her actions.

Both Gilman and Chopin demonstrate how stifling the cult of domesticity was for intelligent women. Throughout "The Yellow Wall-Paper," the narrator, like Chopin's Edna, is at odds with her husband, who seeks to control her behavior and to subdue what he believes to be her overactive imagination. In addition to protracted rest and a specially prescribed diet, a significant part of the narrator's rehabilitation involves the active suppression of her "fancy," which John perceives as "dangerous" (MS, 286–87). If we do a strictly rhetorical analysis of the manuscript, in fact, an intriguing pattern emerges. The story contains ten allusions to the narrator's "fancy" or to her "imaginative power and habit of story making," nine uses of the word "nervous," and only four references to her being "angry." That the narrator emphasizes her nervousness over her wrath suggests that her anger is subordinated to the more pressing concerns about her health, which she believes would improve if she were only allowed to indulge her imagination through writing. But John "hates to have [her] write a word" (MS, 80–81), and the duplicity makes the narrator "very tired" (MS, 49). Along with the prohibition against writing, John usurps power in countless other ways: not only won't he hear of moving into one of the "pretty rooms" downstairs (MS, 106), but he also rejects his wife's appeals to change the wallpaper, refuses to allow her to visit relatives, instructs her to get back into bed, threatens to send her to Dr. Weir Mitchell if she doesn't "pick up faster" (MS, 172), dismisses her concerns about her treatment, and denies her request to return home early. Certainly, then, she has ample cause to be angry with John, who appropriates all power by insisting on her obedience.

Also noteworthy is the narrator's allusion to John's sister, Jennie, who collaborates with John in suppressing the narrator's freedom to write during John's frequent absences. "I mustn't let her find me writing," the narrator remarks. "I verily believe she thinks it is the writing which made me sick!" (MS, 153–55). Although she is "a dear girl," according to the narrator, there is a significant variation in the narrator's depiction of her when we compare the manuscript of the story to its appearance in the *New England Magazine*. In that version, the narrator refers to Jennie as a "perfect and enthusiastic housekeeper" (*NEM*, 166), while in the manuscript copy of the story, the narrator characterizes Jennie as "a perfect—, an enthusiastic—, housekeeper" (MS, 154). The original manuscript reveals a narrator who reassesses her initial description of Jennie as "perfect" and substitutes "enthusiastic," suggesting, perhaps, not only her subconscious resentment of Jennie but also her contempt of the cult of domesticity to which Jennie undoubtedly subscribes. Given the narrator's interest in real "work" (i.e., writing), we can assume that she feels at least some degree of antipathy toward Jennie—the obsequious housekeeper who "hopes for no better profession" (MS, 154–55).

Another cause of the narrator's anger is that John laughs at her, suggesting that he views her as foolish and immature, a point underscored by his reference to her as a "blessed little goose" and a "little girl" (MS, 107, 261). In the fourth paragraph of the story, for example, the narrator writes, "John laughs at me of course, but one expects that in marriage" (MS, 7). The implication is that because of the respective roles they each occupy (his as domineering patriarch, hers as submissive wife), she has come to expect the condescension, insults, and appropriation of power that John exhibits. About a quarter of the way through the story, the narrator remarks that John "laughs at me so about this wallpaper!" (MS, 98–99). At the same time, however, he blames her for her illness, suggesting that she "ought to use [her] will and good sense to check the tendency" to indulge her imagination (MS, 120–21). Immediately, she reiterates her desire to write, remarking that she gets "pretty tired" when she tries. She then turns her attention briefly to the wallpaper, noting that it has a "vicious influence" and that it has "a recurrent spot where the pattern lolls like a broken neck, and two bulbous eyes stare at you upside down" (MS, 129–31). In the next paragraph, she alludes to her anger: "I get positively angry with the impertinence of [the wallpaper]" (MS, 132). The image of the broken neck and bulbous eyes staring at her upside down is a projection of herself, the life that is being choked out of her through John's interdiction, and the fact that her once carefree world has been turned upside down, as a result of her baby's birth. Immediately after her expression of anger, she turns again to a discussion of her imagination, as if to reclaim that which has been forsaken. About three-quarters of the way through the story, John laughs at the narrator for a third time: "He laughed a little the other day and said I seemed to be flourishing in spite of my wall paper" (MS, 342–43). The narrator responds with her own laugh, fearing that John "would make fun of me" or "take me away" if he knew that she were flourishing "because of the wall-paper" (MS, 344–45). But then, even the wallpaper turns malevolent and laughs at her: "And then when the sun came and that awful pattern began to laugh at me I declared I would finish it today!" (MS, 434–35). Her resolve to "finish" the paper evokes another image of anger, since even though she refers to her project of stripping the paper from the walls, another meaning of "finish" is to kill or destroy. The wallpaper becomes animated to the point that "those strangled heads and bulbous eyes and waddling fungus growths just shriek with derision!" and it "just enjoys" tormenting the narrator (MS, 461–62). Finally, even Jennie laughs near the end of the story when she discovers that her sister-in-law has "peeled off yards" of the wallpaper (MS, 432): "She laughed and said she wouldn't mind doing it herself, but I must not get tired. . . . no person touches this paper but me—not alive!" (MS, 440–42). Once again, the laughter elicits in the narrator a sense of rage and an implicit threat to kill anyone who tries to touch "her" paper. Near the end of the story, the narrator reveals that she is "getting angry enough to do something desperate," but she is still rational enough to rule out suicide since it might be "misconstrued" (MS, 463–66). The implication here is that if she takes her life, others might misinterpret her actions as those of a woman who has gone insane. In a last-ditch attempt to get John's attention, the narrator *does* do something desperate: she locks herself into, and crawls around, the wallpapered room. Her actions are both premeditated—she wants "to astonish" John (MS, 454)—and a blatant manifestation of the anger that has been building throughout the summer.

In more subtle ways, too, Gilman's choice of language in the manuscript version—when compared to the 1892 *New England Magazine* printing—reveals a narrator whose word choice, when decoded, suggests a seething—and perhaps subconscious—anger. For example, in the magazine version the narrator reveals that thinking about her "condition" always makes her "feel bad," so she "will let it alone and *talk* about the house" (*NEM*, 33–34, emphasis added). In the manuscript, however, she decides to "let it alone, and *write* about the house" (MS, 31, emphasis added)—a far more defiant act, since it is her writing that meets with "heavy opposition" and has been expressly prohibited (MS, 27). A little later, when the narrator describes the wallpaper pattern, the magazine version reads, "I never saw so much expression in an inanimate thing before, and we all know how much expression they have!" (*NEM*, 146–47). The manuscript, however, reads, "I never saw so much expression in an inanimate thing before, and we all know how much expression inanimate things have!" (MS, 135–37). The plural "they" in the first instance is ambiguous since the antecedent, "an inanimate thing," is singular. In the second instance, however, the repetition of "inanimate thing[s]" assumes significance by functioning as a reflection of the narrator herself. Through his patriarchal dominance, John has tried to render his wife an "inanimate thing"—an object that is lifeless, dull, and free of the "fancies" that he finds "silly" and even "dangerous." She is the objectified "thing" that longs for the "expression" that John tries to suppress, since he believes that her "imaginative power . . . is sure to lead to all manner of excited fancies" and that she should use her "will and good sense to check the tendency" (MS, 119–21). The emphasis through repetition demonstrates her desire to give voice to—and to animate—that which John would prefer to see passive and compliant.

Another variant between the manuscript and the 1892 publication appears when the narrator describes the scene in which she breaks down in tears after John denies her request to "make a visit to Cousin Henry and Julia" (MS, 223). In the *New England Magazine*, John "gathered [the narrator] up in his arms" (*NEM*, 241), while in the manuscript she was "gathered . . . in his *strong* arms" (MS, 228, emphasis added), an implicit reference to the narrator being symbolically strong-armed, or constricted, by John, during the "reasonable talk" in which the narrator attempts to engage him (MS, 222). In a scene that takes place shortly thereafter, the narrator again tries to talk with John, and both the manuscript and the magazine versions report that John dismissed his wife's attempts to discuss her depression with "a stern reproachful look" and the admonition to "never for one instant let <u>that</u> idea [that she is emotionally distraught,] enter [her] mind" (MS, 282–85). The *New England Magazine,* however, reports that immediately following the discussion, "we went to sleep" (*NEM,* 304), while the manuscript notes that "*he* went to sleep" (MS, 288, emphasis added), leaving the narrator wide awake. John's sleep effectively ends the conversation and silences his wife, leaving her unable to make her case. John's brusque dismissal of the narrator's concerns is likely to feed the anger that she harbors as he continues to deny her a voice.

Another variant in the manuscript version is an entire sentence that does not appear in the *New England Magazine.* Among the many ways the narrator characterizes the wallpaper is as "a sickly penetrating suggestive yellow," a subtle allusion to sexual coercion that has resulted in her pregnancy and subsequent depression (MS, 353–54). The "great immovable bed" is, after all, "nailed" to the floor (MS, 186) and becomes a symbol of John's power to demand, at his pleasure, conjugal relations with his wife—a scenario that would likely engender both fear and antipathy in the narrator—since she is already despondent as a consequence of the pregnancy that resulted in the birth of her son.

Once the narrator decides to liberate the captive woman—her symbolic sister in bondage—from behind the wallpaper, she determines, in the manuscript version, to "try tearing it" (MS, 411). The verb "tearing" suggests a dynamic and even aggressive action on the part of the narrator, reinforcing her rejection of the quiet passivity to which John tries to make her conform. In the magazine version, however, the narrator merely notes that she "mean[s] to try it" (*NEM,* 437–38), making the act devoid of the more ferocious "tearing" that she alludes to in the manuscript. Moreover, in the final scene, the manuscript's inclusion of the adjective "strong" (absent from the 1892 publication), when the narrator refers to the "beautiful strong door" that John is threatening to break down with an "ax" (MS, 481–82), can be read as the symbolic (albeit Freudian) door behind which the narrator has barricaded herself not only to indulge her desire to write but also to avoid the sexual servitude that defines, in part, the role of the nineteenth-century wife.

In addition, Gilman encodes John's denial of his wife's illness, which is ample cause for the narrator's resentment, in the title of the story itself. "The Yellow Wall-Paper" is an anagram for "the lowly appear well," and, ironically, to the self-absorbed John, who "does not believe" his wife is sick—that she suffers only "a slight hysterical tendency" (MS, 14–17)—the narrator appears to be improving.[16] A proud and arrogant man, John uses his "high standing" (MS, 15) as a physician to systematically disempower his comparatively "low" wife. He tries to assure her that her health is not "in any danger" and that she really is better, whether she can see it or not (MS, 267). He warns her repeatedly that "there is nothing so dangerous" as indulging a "false and foolish fancy" (MS, 286–87). He also invokes his medical authority by asking her, in apparent exasperation, "Can you not trust me as a physician when I tell you so?" (MS, 287), a clear signal to his wife that the conversation is over. "So of course I said no more on that score," she reports, although she believes she is "not gaining" under the treatment he has prescribed and wishes "he would take [her] away" (MS, 288, 263–64). When he faints at the end of the story, the formerly deferential narrator has managed to deflate the powerful John. She has succeeded—literally and figuratively—in bringing him down to her level. Both through her language—"It is no use, young man"—a correlate to John's earlier characterization of her as a "little girl" (MS, 479, 261)—and her actions, she has knocked John off his lofty pedestal. It is a calculated move on her part, fueled by the rage she feels as a result of John's imperious nature. Rather than an indication that "the narrator has lost her mind," her actions suggest, as Feldstein proposes, that "the protagonist *decides* to seek revenge" against John.[17]

Feldstein argues that to read "'The Yellow Wall-Paper' as simply a flat representation of one woman's progressive descent into insanity is to diagnose the protagonist's case by means of the empirical ontology championed by the protagonist's doctor husband John, her doctor brother, and [the famous nerve specialist] Doctor Weir Mitchell."[18] Hence, with few exceptions, traditionally "feminist" readings of the story ironically reject the possibility that the obviously bright, imaginative, and clearly oppressed woman might become angry enough to retaliate against John by showing how sick and tired she is of the "pattern"—a word used twenty-four times in the story—by which she is systematically disempowered. Her allusion to her husband in the penultimate paragraph of the story as "that man" (MS, 496) suggests the detachment she now feels toward him, resulting from cumulative rage.[19]

Perhaps one of the most compelling arguments to support the narrator's sanity is the lucid and coherent manner in which she continues to chronicle the events that transpire, even after her decidedly unconventional behavior at the end of the story. Although we can't pinpoint the precise juncture at which she switches from journal writing to a stream-of-consciousness narration, she is able to describe episodes (e.g., the tearing down of the wallpaper and the fainting of her husband) that have already taken place. She is also still able to formulate value judgments, not only about the moral implications of suicide, but also about the potential waste of destroying a perfectly good door: "It would be a shame to break that beautiful strong door" (MS, 482), she remarks. How then, if she is insane, as many critics insist, is she able to continue her story? Since insanity is often characterized by some degree of mental confusion, it seems unlikely that an insane narrator would be able to convey a sequence of events in such a logical, orderly, and highly descriptive fashion.[20]

The other compelling argument for declaring the narrator angry, rather than insane, at the story's end is the addition of ninety paragraphs in the *New England Magazine* version. Readers often cite the seemingly rambling nature of the narrative as evidence of the narrator's decline, arguing that the fragmentation in her description of events is analogous to the narrator's broken condition. The manuscript version, however, is far more coherent, providing a comparatively lucid account of events. By way of example, one early paragraph in the manuscript in which the narrator discusses her condition (the paragraph beginning "You see he does not believe I am sick!") becomes four paragraphs in the *New England Magazine*, making the narrator's account in the published version seem considerably more frenzied than in the manuscript, where the paragraph appears intact. Similarly, the single paragraph in the manuscript that describes the odor of the wallpaper becomes five paragraphs in the magazine, creating a disjointed narrative account that casts doubts on the narrator's ability to process sensory data, the stuff of reality. In short, the addition of ninety paragraph breaks grossly distorts what is a fairly cohesive narrative in manuscript.

Finally, I would be remiss if I failed to comment on Gilman's own stated purpose for writing "The Yellow Wall-Paper." In her autobiography, *The Living of Charlotte Perkins Gilman*, she remarks that "the real purpose of the story was to reach Dr. S. Weir Mitchell," the physician who treated her for neurasthenia in 1887, and to "convince him of the error of his ways" in prescribing the rest cure (121).[21] Although Gilman characterized the story as describing a "nervous breakdown beginning something as mine did, and treated as Dr. S. Weir Mitchell treated me with what I considered the inevitable result, progressive insanity" (119), there is little doubt that the story served another purpose—to rail against the husband, Charles Walter Stetson, whom she held partially responsible for her depression. Stetson had been a persistent suitor for two years before Gilman reluctantly agreed to marry him after "he had met a keen personal disappointment" (83). Her own words are telling: "My mind was not fully clear as to whether I should or should not marry . . . I felt strongly that for me it was not right, that the nature of the life before me [i.e., to devote her life to public service] forbade it" (83). A strong-willed woman, she must have resented Stetson's relentless pressure on her to become his wife.

The day before she left to undergo the rest cure in Dr. Mitchell's Philadelphia sanitarium, Gilman blasted her young husband in her private journal:

> I am very sick with nervous prostration. . . . No one can ever know what I have suffered in these last five years. Pain pain pain, till my mind has given way.
>
> O blind and cruel! Can <u>Love</u> hurt like this? . . .
>
> I leave you—O remember what, and learn to doubt your judgement before it seeks to mould another life as it has mine.
>
> I asked you a few days only before our marriage if you would take the responsibility entirely on yourself. You said yes. Bear it then.[22]

Clearly, Gilman blamed her husband—who appears as the thinly disguised John in "The Yellow Wall-Paper"—for "mould[ing]" her life. The anger expressed in her diary is enormous as she holds her husband accountable for the "pain pain pain" she has "suffered in these last five years." Ironically, in the final diary entry made just before her departure for Philadelphia, Gilman invoked images that would later appear in the final paragraphs of "The Yellow Wall-Paper." She alludes to coming home after taking her "baby to Mary's," the same name she gives the nursemaid in her story, and discovering the "doors locked" with "no key to be found." Refusing to be defeated, however, Gilman "struggle[d] in at [the] bay window with much effort," wrote a diary entry, and commenced "to write an account of myself for the doctor." Like the narrator of her story, Gilman found writing was central to her survival.

Interestingly, however, in Gilman's "account" of herself that she wrote for Mitchell, which has recently been recovered, she depicts Stetson as tender and loyal, informing Mitchell, "My husband is devotion itself." Rather than implicating Stetson as the reason for her nervous collapse, she instead indicts the institution of marriage, noting that the "very cheerful disposition" that was hers prior to marriage had been eclipsed by "a mental misery and an accompanying weakness beyond description."[23]

There is little doubt, however, that when he read "The Yellow Wall-Paper," Walter Stetson recognized in John a portrait of himself, and his spouse seemed smugly satisfied by his reaction. In a letter to a longtime friend, Martha Luther Lane, she urged: "When my awful story 'The Yellow Wallpaper' comes out, you must try & read it. Walter says he has read it four times, and thinks it is the most ghastly tale he ever read. . . . But that's only a husband's opinion."[24] Until recently, we had only Gilman's word about her husband's reaction to the story, but there is new evidence to corroborate her account. An offprint copy of the story's 1892 appearance in the *New England Magazine,* obtained by me through private sale, contains the following inscription in Stetson's hand: "This story seems to me a masterpiece! I've read it a half dozen times, first and last, and each time it fairly makes me shudder. Ch[arles]. W. S[tetson]." In the end, the autobiographically inspired indictment of Mitchell's rest cure can be read as a psychological maneuver on Gilman's part: by deflecting conscious criticism away from Walter Stetson, toward whom she felt considerable rage, she also avoided confronting the vulnerable part of herself that had reluctantly submitted to a marriage of servility against her better judgment.[25] Ultimately, the "The Yellow Wall-Paper" is not simply a story about the consequences of the rest cure or a depiction of insanity, but also a bold expression of anger about the throngs of "creeping women" silenced and subjugated by nineteenth-century patriarchy.

Notes

1. M.D., "Perilous Stuff," letter to the editor, *Boston Evening Transcript,* 8 April 1892, 6.

2. See, for example, an anonymous review in the *Boston Daily Advertiser* that the cover of the chapbook edition was meant "to represent the horrible wall covering that caused the insanity of the narrator." (Anon., "New Books and Those Who Make Them," *Boston Daily Advertiser,* 10 June 1899, 8.) Another review in the *Los Angeles Sunday Times* noted that the protagonist attempts to hide "the signs of her insanity." (Anon., "Fresh Literature: Matters of Interest in the World of Letters," *Los Angeles Sunday Times,* 18 June 1899, 14.)

3. See Elaine Hedges, afterword to Charlotte Perkins Gilman, *The Yellow Wall-Paper* (Old Westbury: Feminist Press, 1973), 55.

4. In Catherine Golden, ed., *The Captive Imagination: A Casebook on "The Yellow Wallpaper"* (New York: Feminist Press, 1992), several critics comment on the narrator's insanity. For example, Beate Schöppe-Schilling argues that the narrator "descends into madness" (143); Sandra Gilbert and Susan Gubar comment that "the narrator sinks . . . into what the world calls madness" (146); Annette Kolodny refers to "the wife's progressive descent into madness" (155), to her "liberation only into madness" (158), and to her "isolation into madness" (162); Paula A. Treichler opines that the narrator's madness is both "positive and negative" (198); Jeffrey Berman asserts that the narrator "lose[s] [her] mind" (235); Judith Fetterley declares that the narrator chooses "madness" (258), a charge repeated by Golden (304); Janice Haney-Peritz remarks that the narrator is "in some sense mad" (271); and Mary Jacobus characterizes the narrator as a "mad woman" (292).

5. See Richard Feldstein, "Reader, Text, and Ambiguous Referentiality in 'The Yellow Wallpaper,'" in *Feminism and Psychoanalysis,* ed. Feldstein and Judith Roof (Ithaca: Cornell University Press, 1989); reprinted in Golden, *Captive Imagination,* 307–18.

6. For further discussion of the addition of paragraphs to the *New England Magazine* version, see Shawn St. Jean, "Gilman's Manuscript of 'The Yellow Wall-Paper': Toward a Critical Edition," *Studies in Bibliography* 15 (1998): 272.

7. Gilman quotes Dr. Brummell (elsewhere "Brommell") Jones in an undated typescript located in the Gilman Papers at the Schlesinger Library. She also paraphrases his correspondence in her essay "Why I Wrote 'The Yellow Wallpaper'?" (*Forerunner*, October 1913) and quotes him again in her autobiography, *The Living of Charlotte Perkins Gilman* (New York: D. Appleton-Century Co., 1935; repr., Madison: University of Wisconsin Press, 1991), 120.

8. I have long believed that "Gilman uses madness as a powerful metaphor in the story. 'Madness' manifested as progressive incipient insanity and 'madness' manifested as extreme and repressed anger at female bondage become dichotomous components of the protagonist's condition." Knight, introduction to *"The Yellow Wall-Paper" and Selected Stories of Charlotte Perkins Gilman*, ed. Denise D. Knight (Newark: University of Delaware Press, 1994), 16.

9. Feldstein, "Reader, Text," 311–13.

10. Parenthetical references to Gilman's manuscript (MS) and the *New England Magazine* (*NEM*) refer to line numbers of the critical texts printed in this edition.

11. Feldstein, "Reader, Text" 313, emphasis added. Less convincing is Feldstein's argument that Gilman's variant spellings of the word *wallpaper* (as "wallpaper," "wall-paper" and "wall paper") in the manuscript version of the story "were conceived as a shifter calculated to create ambiguity about a referent that resists analysis" (308). Gilman was a notoriously careless writer whose haste caused spelling inconsistencies even, at times, within the same paragraph. In a diary entry for November 19, 1883, for example, she spelled the name of a close friend as both "Carrie" and "Carry." Also noteworthy is Gilman's frequent variant spelling of daughter Katharine's name as "Katherine" in the months following her birth.

But see "Editorial Emendations to the Copy-Texts" in this volume for a purely bibliographic explanation.

12. Elizabeth Ammons, "Writing Silence: 'The Yellow Wallpaper,'" in *The Yellow Wallpaper*, ed. Thomas L. Erskine and Connie L. Richards (New Brunswick, NJ: Rutgers University Press, 1993), 263.

13. Ibid. Like most critics, however, Ammons also contends that "by the end [of the story] the narrator has lost her mind" (264–65).

14. Parenthetical references are to page numbers in "The Revolt of 'Mother,'" *Selected Stories of Mary E. Wilkins Freeman*, ed. Marjorie Pryse (New York: Norton, 1983).

15. Page 61. Parenthetical references are to page numbers in Kate Chopin, *The Awakening* (New York: Signet, 1976).

16. In the nineteenth century, the word *hysteria* (Greek *hystera* = womb) was used rather loosely and was thought to be caused by abnormalities in a woman's reproductive system. The Victorian view of females as weak, fragile, and childlike reinforced this belief. Noncompliance with traditional gender-based roles was often ascribed to hysteria as well.

17. Ammons, "Writing Silence," 265; Feldstein, "Reader, Text," 313, emphasis added.

18. Feldstein, "Reader, Text," 312.

19. Also noteworthy is Gilman's poem "Locked Inside" (1910), which repeats several of the images and thematic threads found in "The Yellow Wall-Paper." *"Herland," "The Yellow Wall-Paper," and Selected Writings of Charlotte Perkins Gilman*, ed. Denise D. Knight. (New York: Penguin, 1999),

339. The oppressed speaker discovers that she possesses the power to alter her condition rather than remain a victim to circumstances:

> She beats upon her bolted door,
>   With faint weak hands;
> Drearily walks the narrow floor;
> Sullenly sits, blank walls before;
>   Despairing stands.   .
>
> Life calls her, Duty, Pleasure, Gain—
>   Her dreams respond;
> But the blank daylights wax and wane,
> Dull peace, sharp agony, slow pain—
>   No hope beyond.
>
> Till she comes a thought! She lifts her head, [sic]
>   The world grows wide!
> A voice—as if clear words were said—
> "Your door, o long imprisoned,
>   Is locked inside!"

Like the narrator of "The Yellow Wall-Paper," the despondent speaker of the poem apparently finds a solution to her subjugation through the realization that she does have the ability to effect change—an epiphany experienced by the narrator when she realizes that in order to make John acknowledge her despair, she "must get to work" (MS, 451)—a undeniably rebellious act, considering that "work" is the one thing she has been "absolutely forbidden to" do (MS, 20).

20. Some critics do suggest that by the end of the story, the narrator is no longer writing at all. For example, Feldstein believes that "a written transcription" is "inexplicably interrupted and succeeded by a spoken account" at some point in the narrative. He argues that late in the story, "the narrator asserts she is speaking to us, not writing in her journal, as she had previously." As evidence, he cites the line, "I have found out another funny thing, but I shan't tell it this time!" (MS, 412. Feldstein, "Reader, Text," 315. In the *New England Magazine* version of the story, however, the narrator states, very early in the story, that she will "*talk* about the house," (*NEM*, 34, emphasis added), a point that complicates the assertion that a narrative shift occurs from written to spoken discourse.

21. Neurasthenia, a term no longer in scientific use, was defined as an emotional and psychological disorder characterized by easy fatigability and often by lack of motivation, feelings of inadequacy, and psychosomatic symptoms. The condition was thought to be caused by exhaustion of the nervous system. Parenthetical references are to page numbers in Gilman, *Living*.

22. All quotations are from Gilman, *The Diaries of Charlotte Perkins Gilman*, ed. Denise D. Knight, 2 vols. (Charlottesville: University Press of Virginia, 1994), 1:385.

23. Until recently, Gilman's 1887 letter to Dr. S. Weir Mitchell was presumed to be either lost or destroyed. The letter has been languishing in obscurity in the archives of the Wisconsin Historical Society since July 1944, when it was donated by William L. Breese, husband of the late American writer Zona Gale (1874–1938), in whose possession the letter had been since shortly before Gilman's death in 1935. For further information about the history and recovery of the letter,

see my article, "'All the facts of the case': Gilman's 'Lost' Letter to Dr. S. Weir Mitchell," in *American Literary Realism* 37 (Spring 2005): 259–77.

24. Gilman [then Stetson] to Lane, July 27, 1890, Rhode Island Historical Society.

25. The treatment that the narrator undergoes in this story is actually a modified rest cure and allows the patient far more liberty than what was typically granted to the nervous invalid. The traditional rest cure required that the patient undertake total bed rest and endure spoon feeding, sponge baths, and total isolation from relatives.

Crazy Writing and Reliable Text

Allan H. Pasco

THE RELIABILITY OF Charlotte Perkins Gilman's first-person narrator, ostensibly an unnamed woman secretly inscribing her journal, has frequently been interrogated by both scholars and lay readers. "Put simply," write Jeanette King and Pam Morris, "the question is whether the woman is seen as sane enough for her testimony to be taken at face value."[1] Their phrase, "seen as," far from superfluous, is crucial and paradoxical for it complicates matters immediately, splitting our critical attention between the *narrator*, who does the writing and speaking, and the *reader*, who does—or does not do—the "seeing" and "taking." And further splits occur, clearly requiring a conscious distinction between Gilman's culture and our own. Much had changed between Gilman's original writing and her late twentieth-century feminist critics, in both their understanding of human psychology and of literature itself. Gilman neither composed nor published this tale in a vacuum. She issued it in the 1890s, a period of psychological realism, when readers of authors from Edgar Allan Poe to Mark Twain were long conditioned to look askance at narrators. "Self-conscious" and "unreliable" narrators were indeed so common that any alert reader of the day would have had to wonder, Is this an account of a madwoman putting pen to paper? Even thirty years later, Sigmund Freud's influence had sophisticated American audiences enough so that the very terms of the question would have changed: Can one give credence to someone who, beginning with a mild nervous disorder called a neurosis, is progressively overtaken by a more severe form of mental and behavioral disturbance, or psychosis? And what other conditions affect the narrator's truthfulness? One of these conditions, a significant one, may lie outside the story: to what extent did the ways in which Gilman's manuscript was altered for publication revise, in general terms, its point of view?

Resolving these questions takes more than a close textual reading of the story. Just as standard formalist practice would insist attention be paid to the "ironic distance" between author, narrator, and character (who even when demonstrably related, as here, are never identical), we must be mindful of our cultural distance from those who habitually called people who departed from accepted behavior mad. Aided by historical and bibliographic knowledge, we can begin with an expanded diagnosis of the specific affliction Gilman invested in her narrator. It is today known as postpartum depression and psychosis.[2]

Some maladies were understood in the nineteenth and even the eighteenth centuries as mentally connected to childbirth and its aftermath. Postpartum psychological disorders were nonetheless grouped with hysteria, a vague and generalized category that included other varieties of nervous prostration and neurasthenia. The diarist's symptoms in "The Yellow Wall-Paper" could appropriately have been included with Louis Victor Marcé's meticulous description in 1858 of forty-four cases of serious psychological illness after birth.[3] Medical people hoped that a treatment capable of controlling the symptoms, when combined with counseling, would bring healing. Some cures attempted to use opiates, barbiturates, and antipsychotic and antidepressant drugs as the preferred means of damping down the undesirable mental aberrations that resemble severe depression or schizophrenia. Alternatively, physician S. Weir Mitchell, later to become Gilman's nemesis, developed a "rest cure" consisting of depriving patients of stimulation. Though he was successful in arousing interest and attracting patients (including notables like Edith Wharton), there is no evidence that he was particularly effective in curing the disease. Gilman believed, contrarily, that only productive work held hope for healing. Since the 1960s, however, some physicians have suggested that depression's relationship to childbirth offers a signal indication of its difference from symptomatically similar diseases: it is hormonal—that is, physiological (a condition of the body) as well as psychological (a condition of the mind)—in nature.

Mild depression after the birth of a child is now acknowledged as quite common. In most cases, it is nothing but a few days of "the blues." But when the depression continues and deepens for a lengthier period, it should be treated by administering balancing hormones, for it can become a very serious derangement.

Postpartum psychosis, an extreme exacerbation of postpartum depression, has been estimated to occur after something like one delivery in a thousand. The American Psychiatric Association's *Diagnostic and Statistical Manual of Mental Disorders-IV* recognizes this advanced form of the malady and lists a range of symptoms that indicate its presence (not all of which need to be present for a diagnosis): an inability to concentrate, insomnia, significant weight gain or loss, confusion, mania, obsessive thoughts, delusions, severe anxiety, and panic attacks. Spontaneous crying is also common, since such new mothers feel worthless and guilty about being depressed despite the birth of a wonderful infant. Persistent aural, visual, olfactory, and tactile hallucinations frequently occur, as do bouts of amnesia. The illness generally requires hospitalization and close supervision, for it can result in suicide. Given that maternal feelings are commonly either overwhelmed by the symptoms or lacking, it can in rare cases lead to infanticide.[4] In "The Yellow Wall-Paper," John and his wife disagree about whether she is gaining or losing weight, but with this possible exception, and that of panic attacks, the scribe of Gilman's account exhibits every symptom.

The unnamed narrator has recently given birth and represents a classic case of deepening postpartum depressive psychosis. Symptom by salient symptom, with scientifically accurate reporting, the scribe's text follows her into an extreme state of mental derangement that can legitimately be termed insanity. A vital point: on this (paradoxical) level, she *is* a reliable narrator, for her narration accurately portrays her illness. While the distortions, the hallucinations, the obsessions may not be exact representations of exterior reality, they *are* astonishingly accurate accounts of what could occur in the mind of someone suffering from postpartum psychosis, enabled by Gilman's personal experience of the disease and her almost certain acquaintance with others who were similarly afflicted. It is at this level, then, that the issue of reliability is most usefully engaged.

The story slowly builds to a crescendo of psychological anguish through a variety of linguistic subtleties. For instance, an armature of oppositions belies the purported solicitude John has for his wife, their ability to communicate with each other, and the equality of their relationship. The narrator in Gilman's phrase "John and I" (MS, 1) is demoted to "John and myself" in the magazine's first line.[5] Though the husband laughs and talks, the narrator weeps and keeps silent in his presence. He works at meaningful employment, while she is encouraged to do nothing and is even ordered not to "work." In manuscript, the voice clearly announces an intention to "write" (while he is not present) about the house (MS, 31). The change of that word to "talk" (*NEM*, 34) maintains an ambiguity concerning her obedience to John's prohibition much later into the narrative. Is she writing or talking? In at least one case, she bursts into tears while trying to converse with John. He is reasonable, practical, well, and energetic, though she is whimsical, sick, and fatigued. He is clearly an adult, and she regresses to childhood and infancy.

And like many Western writers, Gilman understood how to exploit the symbolism and connotative language of what Carl Jung would later call the collective unconscious. A mansion, for example, is a common literary device for representing the individual, mind and body; among legions of works, one might think of the relationship between Roderick Usher and the "House of Usher" (1839). Unlike Poe, however, Gilman was not a romantic, though her narrator is a thwarted one: in "The Yellow Wall-Paper," the house dominates the initial paragraphs, where the diarist notes, as well, that it might even be haunted. She'd *like* it to be haunted, that is, though "that would be asking too much of fate!" (*NEM*, 4). The deflation here is echoed by the clinging to enthusiastic vagary in "anyhow, it has been empty for years and years" (MS, 42) being revised to defeatist precision in "anyhow, the place has been empty for years" (*NEM*, 44). Clearly, then, in *NEM*, the narrator's depression is not a function of a rampant imagination. The more chilling fact, from the standpoint of realism—that she is but a temporary resident—emphasizes that she is an outsider, an alien where she should be most at home. Her husband had rented the residence while repairs were being made to their own abode. Lone and displaced romantic characters, defeated or destroyed, were a staple of realist fiction like that of James, Wharton, and Crane. In fact, although it invokes some well-established conventions of romance, Gilman's is far more a story than a tale, more reliant on the commonplace and natural than the gothic and supernatural. Repeated mentions of "ancestral halls," and "colonial mansion[s]" (*NEM*, 1–3) might recall the slavery prevalent earlier in the century. The "hereditary estate" (*NEM*, 3; the reader may further recollect Hawthorne's *The House of the Seven Gables* [1851]), rather than invoking ghosts, deftly suggests the possibility of genetic instability that will be both dominated and confined, and it sets up a shadowy double that the heroine sees in the wallpaper. At first, she thinks it the spirit of some bygone sufferer. Only weeks later does she recognize it as her own doppelgänger. What the *reader* makes of this apparition, remains to be seen.

The scribe assumes that the ominous room was once furnished for children, first as a nursery, then as a playroom. These were singularly violent children, seemingly: "I never saw such ravages as the children have made here. . . . the floor is scratched and gouged and splintered, the plaster itself is dug out here and there, and this great heavy bed . . . looks as if it had been through the wars" (*NEM*, 156–62). Her associations of youngsters with destruction should be juxtaposed to her declaration that her own is "such a dear baby" (*NEM*, 102), and yet she has relinquished his care to a woman (Mary) given far fewer credentials than even the housekeeper (*NEM*, 102), showing the extent of her repressed fear and perhaps guilt as an abandoning mother. In actuality, the barred windows, the "rings and things in the walls" (*NEM*, 69), "that great bedstead nailed down" (*NEM*, 477), and "then that gate at the head of the stairs" (*NEM*, 110), not to mention the "hedges and walls and gates that lock" (*NEM*, 37), all bespeak another history, that of an adult being restrained for the protection of herself and others.

At first the diarist is compelled to write about her experience with the old house, although it tires her: "I *must* say what I feel and think in some way—it is such a relief" (*NEM*, 228–29). The relief soon costs more effort than it is worth, however; without permanently discontinuing the activity of writing, the diarist commits herself to an increasingly passionate study of the yellow wallpaper. By writing in her diary, she disobeys her husband. As she writes less and less, she feels more and more in subjection. The *New England Magazine* text subtly underlines this feeling by changing the "on"s of the manuscript ("the low sun shines directly on it" and "[the pattern] knocks you down and tramples on you"; MS, 207, 299) to "upon" (*NEM*, 220, 315). Writing leads directly to the hallucinations that assail her and that the text legitimizes by providing a written record. She turns her eyes from the pages of her diary to wallpaper that she "follow[s]" (*NEM*, 203) and "watch[es]" (*NEM*, 255). "There are things in that paper that nobody knows but me," she says (*NEM*, 256). First she discerns "sprawling flamboyant patterns committing every artistic sin" (*NEM*, 74), curves that "suddenly commit suicide" (*NEM*, 77), and one "recurrent spot where the pattern lolls like a broken neck and two bulbous eyes stare at you upside down" (*NEM*, 140–41). For a while, it seems "a kind of 'debased Romanesque' with *delirium tremens*" (*NEM*, 210), then it resembles "great slanting waves of optic horror" (*NEM*, 213) that become "toadstools" (*NEM*, 317) and "fungus" (*NEM*, 370).[6] Thoughts of jumping out the window afflict her, "but the bars are too strong even to try. Besides, I wouldn't do it of course! I know well enough that a step like that is improper" (MS, 464–66). The "I wouldn't do it of course!" (MS, 465) becomes "I wouldn't do it. Of course not." (*NEM*, 499), a revision that positively reverses the direction here, introducing a second, more rational but momentary thought by the manic narrator. By this point, the visions that fill the scribe's diary have taken readers progressively farther from normal reality, irretrievably into psychosis, in a grotesque world governed by morbidity and thoughts of suicide.

The symptoms that we recognize as an accurately conveyed postpartum disorder include fatigue, but fatigue often accompanied by insomnia. Though the scribe continues to study the wallpaper: "I lie down ever so much now. John says it is good for me, and to sleep all I can" (*NEM*, 334). Of course, she explains, "I don't sleep much at night, for it is so interesting to watch developments; but I sleep a good deal in the daytime" (*NEM*, 367–68). She disagrees with her husband that sleep is helpful, and the reader is implicitly encouraged to wonder whether she might not be more active at night than she says, or remembers (amnesia commonly occurs with postpartum disorders). The later discovery while creeping that her "shoulder just fits in that long smooch around the wall" (*NEM*, 512–13) might imply that she has been nocturnally creeping and creating the "smooch" well before she consciously realizes it. Visual hallucinations increase, and olfactory hallucinations begin. "I find [the smell] hovering in the dining-room, skulking in the parlor, hiding in the hall, lying in wait for me on the stairs" (*NEM*, 380–81). And, reminiscent of Maupassant's "Le Horla" (1887), she thinks "seriously of burning the house—to reach the smell" (*NEM*, 391–92).

Finally, in the wallpaper, the diarist discerns "a woman stooping down and creeping about behind that pattern" (*NEM*, 259–60). The "border" of the early version (MS, 204) was changed to a "frieze" (*NEM*, 217), I suspect as a focal point for subsequent hallucinations, indicating depth for all the things going on behind the surface. With the terrible rhythm of a relentless crescendo, the images of this ghostly woman recur as the narrator's personal involvement is emphasized. From the standpoint of Freudian psychology, the fleeting glimpses of the imagined prisoner caught in the vines of the wallpaper pattern serve the heroine to *displace* her self-pity. The nebulously "unpleasant" (MS, 399) need to hide becomes psychically "humiliating" (*NEM*, 424) in the magazine text, as a further refinement of unwanted emotions. The pathetic wraith she glimpses in the wallpaper seems to shake the pattern, as though she wants to escape, and the heroine distinguishes between the dimensional depths of the paper. There appears to be a front and back, an outside and inside pattern. Behind that on the outside, "as plain as can be" (*NEM*, 329), a woman creeps—perhaps any number of women. Others have attempted escape from the bars, but "the pattern strangles them off and turns them upside down, and makes their eyes white!" (*NEM*, 411–12). When the diarist finally begins to actively resist what is happening to her, she attacks the wallpaper (a target displacing her hatred for John and his confinements). As a result, she believes she has freed other women, for outdoors she sees "so many of those creeping women, and they creep so fast" (*NEM*, 501–2). She works with her double: "I pulled and she shook, I shook and she pulled, and before morning we had peeled off yards of that paper" (*NEM*, 460–61). Then, like other women who have been forced by a patriarchal, medical culture into infantile roles, she begins to creep "round and round and round" the room (*NEM*, 399). For an adult to take such a role is, of course, mentally aberrant; at this point the diary's author might seem "simply crazy."

And yet the story has prepared us early for all these mental displacements with physical ones: the narrator taking the baby's place in the bedroom, "I can stand it so much easier than a baby" (*NEM*, 253)—a memory brought on by John's carrying her up the stairs like an infant and reading to her; the displacement of the narrator by Mary in the mothering role (*NEM*, 102); and most important, the resulting ambivalence and revulsion caused by physical contact with the baby. "Such a dear baby! And yet I *cannot* be with him, it makes me so nervous" (*NEM*, 102–3); this revulsion is aggravated by subconscious recognition that the male child will succeed his father as a privileged patriarch. Would continued contact deepen resentment into hostility, introducing impulses toward infanticide that the narrator instead less guiltily displaces toward suicide later? Common displacements might otherwise be called unconscious coping strategies, the mind attempting to protect one from recognition of the "badness" in oneself; in short, neuroses, the healthy form of more uncontrolled psychoses. But the impulse to harm others, displaced onto oneself—today often seen in self-mutilations—tells us we are in the company not of a lunatic but of a neurotic devolved into a psychotic.

Creeping, an action that recalls both the plants perceived in the wallpaper and the normal movement of a baby, has three important functions: it suggests the writer's infantile state; it insists on her subordinate position; and, in the conclusion, it changes to suggest the beginning of self-assertion, thus of healing. For babies, creeping is a positive activity that accompanies the child's progression toward independence. The three interpretations are viscerally related, though the relationship may not be apparent before the end. From the outset, we learn that the heroine is subordinate to men and to doctors; both her husband and her brother are physicians. They say "the same thing" (*NEM*, 20–21). True, the narrator points to John's love on several occasions ("Dear John! He loves me very dearly"; *NEM*, 234), but for all his affection, his inability to understand her makes him seem cruel.

As the writer reverts increasingly to outwardly docile childhood, more often than not alone in the bedroom, increasingly supine, she accepts a world separated into "them" and "me." She believes her healing will come only when she succeeds in letting her double out, which happens near the end, though there is only the suggestion that they conjoin into one being. She determines to understand the wallpaper. By insisting on thought, she thus consciously resists her husband and his sister, Jennie, who "sees to everything now" (*NEM*, 183). The resistance is significant, since it is a clear signal that she no longer accepts the role being imposed on her. Finally she assaults the wallpaper, pulling it from the wall as high as she can reach. And she pursues her infantile creeping. Linda Wagner-Martin calls it "the greatest indignity: the mother of the child becomes the child, the 'little girl' of the household."[7] Nonetheless, in the midst of this apparent dementia, the diarist provides evidence that she has arranged the path of her own liberation. She has locked her door and thrown the key "down by the front steps, under a plantain leaf" (*NEM*, 519–20). The plantain was believed to symbolize self-education.[8] Perhaps John is being forced to learn about his wife. Perhaps she has learned about herself. This dramatic event throws a number of preceding passages into relief. The physical descriptions of the prisonlike house have encouraged readers to pass over the fact that she is not locked in her room (until she does it herself), she is not tied to the rings in the walls, and is not hindered by the gates, for she goes for walks and rides. She could consequently have been freed earlier by exercising her will, as she finally does. John retrieves the key and unlocks the door.

John has already threatened to send her to Weir Mitchell in the fall. She has no illusion of good results from such treatment, since her friend "who was in his hands once, . . . says he is just like John and my brother, only more so!" (*NEM*, 186–87). It seems reasonable to assume that when John arises from his faint he will attempt to force her to pursue the Mitchell "cure." Will the scribe end her life locked away in some attic? On the basis of what we know about Gilman's experience of the Mitchell rest cure, there is little room for optimism. Neither the story nor Gilman's autobiography would encourage us to believe that enforced idleness would have anything but disastrous results. Of course, should the story's conclusion be read in terms of Gilman's life, there might well be cause for hope. Gilman, after all, rejected Mitchell's prescription as she (with daughter Katharine) left her husband and found her healing in a combination of work and personal freedom. Although recurring depression plagued her for much of her life, it is quite clear from today's medical understanding that Gilman eventually began to function normally, apparently restored to something approaching endocrinal equilibrium and its accompanying physical and psychological normalcy. Might a reader suspect that the heroine of "The Yellow Wall-Paper" will likewise have a similar, spontaneous restoration?

Even if we reject the intervention of external contexts and read the story as carefully as the heroine studies the wallpaper, there is textual reason to believe in a healthy future. Perhaps most significant in the concluding dozen lines is the predominance of verbs in the past tense: "That silenced him," "said I," "then I said it again," "and he got it," "I had to creep over him" (*NEM*, 521–32). The fact that the diarist, who was silenced, is able to report after the events argues that something positive has happened after her apparent breakdown at the close of the story. Before this point, the carefully controlled dominant tense is the present, as the scribe communicates to the "dead paper" (*NEM*, 13) of her journal what is going on in her mind and life. In the case, however, of the inappropriate past tense of "I wonder if they all came out" (*MS*, 469) the magazine version has been rectified to read, "I wonder if they all come out of that wall-paper" (*NEM*, 503). The present tense record of her increasing passivity, irrationality, and submission to John is coun- terbalanced by the concluding, contrary, after-the-fact account of her scriptorial revolt against authority and by her actions to silence and overcome her husband. An alien hand is surely responsible for altering the "I get positively angry" of both manuscript and magazine (MS, 132; *NEM*, 142) to "I got positively angry" in the Small, Maynard book of 1899. Likewise, "how I wish" (MS, 222–23; *NEM*, 235–36) mysteriously became "wished" in Small, Maynard. Appropriate use of the strate- gically placed present tense is essential to set off and highlight the consequently surprising past tenses of the conclusion and thus provides a reason to believe that the author was not involved with editions after *NEM*.

Just as the writer's original change from walking, to sitting at the window, to becoming nocturnal, to spending increasing time in bed is discouraging—for it parallels her psychotic disintegration—so her standing to tear off the wallpaper appears encouraging and constructive. Degeneration of the brain is checked by stimulation of the body. Today we know that exercise raises the release of sero- tonin and other neurotransmitters to the brain, directly countering effects of fear, anxiety, insomnia, fatigue, and depression brought on by low levels of those neuro- transmitters. In fact, a close comparison of final pages of the original manuscript to the revised magazine printing reveals a woman who has become both men- tally and physically stronger: she is able to articulate longer phrases and complete thoughts, as in the change from "servants, and the things" (MS, 446) to "servants are gone, and the things are gone" (*NEM*, 476) and from "do it of course!" (MS, 465) to "do it. Of course not" (*NEM*, 499). She actually has strength to attempt to "lift *and* push" the bed (*NEM*, 492, emphasis added) and to creep *repeatedly* over John (*NEM*, 532). Finally, her appraisal of the door as merely "beautiful" (*NEM*, 518) rather than "strong" (MS, 482) alerts us to her sense of her own increased power. The activity and energy she displays in rising from her bed, and the rebellion that leads her to rip off the offensive wall covering are in direct opposition to the stric- tures of her dominating, authoritarian husband and physician: "'I've got out at last,' said I, 'in spite of you and Jane! And I've pulled off most of the paper, so you can't put me back!'" (*NEM*, 529–30).[9] She is in the process of gaining victory over her internal confusion and her situation: the enforced regimen, her physician hus- band and his sister, and the threat of Dr. S. Weir Mitchell. If so, the creeping no longer signifies madness alone, but in addition calls to mind a baby's crawling to- ward self-affirmation and independence.

When John unlocks the door and sees his wife creeping, his response is to faint, an unquestionable example of shock and weakness, thus revealing "feminine" susceptibilities. As Ann Douglas Wood puts it, *"He* has become the woman, the nervous, susceptible, sickly patient."[10] His wife "had to creep over him" (*NEM,* 532) as she circles the room. The regressive movement toward dementia and infancy may have been reversed in the final lines of the story, for after working to pull off the wallpaper, the heroine announces her liberty and devotes herself to an activity that raises her physically above the prostrated husband. The rise is probably permanent, as indicated by the magazine's addition of "every time" to the ending (*NEM,* 532). Because the scribe is able to write the last few lines of the story in retrospect and in the past tense, we are left implicit hope that she will continue to resist the oppressive world within and around her and pursue what she only vaguely understands to be the stuff of healing: the engagement of work and intellectual and physical stimulation that she has yearned for from the beginning.

On reading "The Yellow Wall-Paper," no one can fail to be impressed with the many indications of depression, the suggestion of a lack of maternal feelings, the passing references to suicide, to amnesia, to fatigue, to sadness, confusion, a lack of pleasure and joy, weight loss, impaired psychomotor activity, diminished ability to think, the continuing insomnia, and, of course, the description of overpowering visual and olfactory hallucinations. Today's specialists would not hesitate to recognize this as a reliable representation of severe postpartum psychosis, though they would probably not be so sanguine about the healing of a patient with the help of neither therapy nor hormones nor psychotropic medications. The disease tends to become deeply ingrained and chronic when untreated. However, Gilman herself was treated—by composition and revision of her account—and thus did the work of what Freud called self-therapy.

Because her representations are so incredibly accurate, readers may become conscious of a second story, where women are so dominated by sovereign males at every level, from body to mind, that they begin to suppress their own traits as individual, thinking adults. Perhaps this explains why the scribe is from start to finish bereft of a name. The narrator doubles, then multiplies, then fragments as she comes close to losing her individuality. Gilman's culture lacked the medical vocabulary and skill to diagnose her malady and quantify her experiences following the birth of her daughter: their opinions were raw ("madness," "hysteria") and the remedies primitive. In order to advance knowledge and treatment—to "save people from being driven crazy," as she put it[11]—Gilman painstakingly documented the case, in the process revising and refining events from her own life to create a *tableau vivant,* a living picture that contributed importantly to the progress of medicine as well as women's literature.

Notes

1. Jeanette King and Pam Morris, "On Not Reading between the Lines: Models of Reading in 'The Yellow Wallpaper,'" *Studies in Short Fiction* 26 (1989): 23.

2. Dale Bauer collates published nineteenth-century medical opinions on what was then called "puerperal mania" in her "cultural edition." Charlotte Perkins Gilman, *The Yellow Wallpaper*, ed. Dale M. Bauer (Boston: Bedford Books, 1998), esp. 171–88.

3. Louis Victor Marcé, *Traité de la folie des femmes enceintes, des nouvelles accouchées et des nourices, et considérations médico-légales qui se rattache à ce sujet* (Paris: J. B. Baillière, 1858).

4. I am particularly indebted to the late Glenn O. Bair, M.D., who specialized in PMS and related female hormone imbalances, for sharing his knowledge and experience with me. For a brief history of the related states of postpartum psychosis, see James Alexander Hamilton, "The Identity of Postpartum Psychosis," in *Motherhood and Mental Illness*, ed. I. F. Brockington and R. Kumar (London: Academic Press, 1982), 1–16. Katharina Dalton and Wendy M. Holton have had success administering natural progesterone. Dalton, with Holton, *Depression after Childbirth: How to Recognize, Treat, and Prevent Postnatal Depression*, 3d ed. (Oxford: Oxford University Press, 1996). For other work on the disease, see American Psychiatric Association, *Diagnostic and Statistical Manual of Mental Disorders: DSM-IV*, 4th ed. (Washington, DC: American Psychiatric Press, 1994); James Alexander Hamilton and Patricia Neel Harberger, eds., *Postpartum Psychiatric Illness: A Picture Puzzle* (Philadelphia: University of Pennsylvania Press, 1992); A. J. P. Gregoire, R. Kumar, B. Everitt, A. F. Henderson, and J. W. W. Studd, "Transdermal Oestrogen for Treatment of Severe Postnatal Depression," *Lancet* 347 (April 6, 1996): 930–33; Kathryn A. Leopold and Lauren B. Zoschnick, "Postpartum Depression," *Female Patient* 22 (September 1997): 12–20.

Although postpartum depression and psychosis seem far and away the best account for the symptoms the diarist suffers, other, more physiologically based explanations have been offered. See, for example, Beth Sutton-Ramspeck's *Raising the Dust* (Athens: Ohio University Press, 2004), in which she explains how the narrator "is sickened not only mentally and emotionally by her confinement but physically by the house itself" (123). At the turn of the century, wallpaper's toxicity due to its arsenic content was warned against in many domestic advice manuals. Among the symptoms that can be ascribed to arsenic poisoning, the narrator experiences excessive crying, great depression, and loss of sleep (124). Even the mysterious, damp smell, its proneness to rub off on clothing, and its very color are consistent details suggesting Gilman, as a literary realist, chose wallpaper as her central motif to at least buttress the generally poisonous environment of the story.

5. *NEM*, line 1. Parenthetical references to Gilman's manuscript (MS) and the *New England Magazine* (*NEM*) refer to line numbers of the critical texts printed in this edition.

The narrator, contrary to common belief among readers, is not unreliable as a character on the grounds I establish, and *NEM* is not unreliable as a text. Although I believe the manuscript's sentence, "A sickly penetrating suggestive yellow," fits into the logic of the creation and that the deletion in *NEM* must have been accidental, I agree with Julie Bates Dock's theory that Gilman must have had something to do with either an intermediary, second copy sent (but now lost) to the *New England Magazine* or with proofing the version published in 1892. *Charlotte Perkins Gilman's "The Yellow Wall-paper" and the History of Its Publication and Reception*, ed. Julie Bates Dock (University Park: Pennsylvania State University Press, 1998), 46–50. It seems to me that *NEM*'s changes improve the story, not only by its greater precision of (psychotic) grammar, diction, and description, but by its awareness of the subtle but essential development of subjection and psychosis in the story. Shawn St. Jean argues, against Dock, that Gilman was not involved with proofing *NEM*. St. Jean, "Gilman's Manuscript of 'The Yellow Wall-Paper': Toward a Critical Edition," *Studies in Bibliography* 51 (1998): 259–73.

6. Rae Beth Gordon considers late nineteenth-century interior decoration and psychiatric studies, and while observing that the story's decorative arabesques reflect the subject's hysteria, she points out that they were, in the period, thought to encourage hallucination—"Interior Decoration in Poe and Gilman," *Lit* 3, no. 2 (1991): 94–96.

7. Linda Wagner-Martin, "Gilman's 'The Yellow Wallpaper': A Centenary," in *Charlotte Perkins Gilman: The Woman and Her Work,* ed. Sheryl L. Meyering (Ann Arbor: UMI Research Press, 1989), 59.

8. Ernst Lehner and Johanna Lehner, *Folklore and Symbolism of Flowers, Plants and Trees* (New York: Tudor, 1960), 123.

9. Jane is not, as William Veeder believes, the name of the heroine, who remains anonymous to the end. Veeder, "Who Is Jane? The Intricate Feminism of Charlotte Perkins Gilman," *Arizona Quarterly* 44 (Autumn 1988): 64–65. Although Jennie is today considered a short form of Jennifer, it was long used as a pet name for Jane. Patrick Hanks and Flavia Hodges, *A Dictionary of First Names* (Oxford: Oxford University Press, 1990), 175. In the late nineteenth century, Jennie was still considered a substitute for Jane. The Jane referred to here is John's sister, usually called Jennie. It is hardly surprising that the narrator would abandon the pet name at this point, in her triumph over her guardians. See also Charlotte M. Yonge, *History of Christian Names* (1884; repr., Detroit: Gale, 1966), 44–46.

10. Wood, from "'The Fashionable Diseases': Women's Complaints and Their Treatment in Nineteenth-Century America," in *The Captive Imagination: A Casebook on "The Yellow Wallpaper,"* ed. Catherine Golden (New York: Feminist Press, 1992), 117, emphasis in original.

11. Gilman, "Why I Wrote 'The Yellow Wallpaper'?" in Golden, *Captive Imagination,* 51–53.

"Another thing/Something else about that paper . . ."

DECONSTRUCTING TEXTS

Shawn St. Jean

"THE YELLOW WALL-PAPER" ends in a puzzling yet sensational fashion: the un-named narrator, whose husband John has just burst into her attic bedroom, announces triumphantly to him (according to the original *New England Magazine* publication) "I've got out at last . . . in spite of you and Jane? And I've pulled off most of the paper, so you can't put me back!"[1]

Already we see that texts of works can cause trouble.[2] The story's climax is enigmatic enough without that inappropriate question mark confusing things further. Editor Leslie Rabkin, who reprinted the *New England Magazine* text in his 1966 collection *Psychopathology and Literature,* proved himself unique among editors by refusing to silently change the punctuation mark to a period or exclamation point. He footnoted the passage: "'Jane?' in the original text. The '?' may have been a printer's effort to warn proofreaders of a possible error. 'Jane' may be the narrator. Or 'Jennie' may be intended."[3] Rabkin's proffered explanations for the "?" seem plausible enough, especially given the evidence of Gilman's original manuscript, which shows that she did not intend interrogative punctuation, but instead used an exclamation point. Perhaps the magazine's compositor misread the mark because of haste or carelessness, or because he anticipated finishing the job on this eccentric story, or for some other unrecoverable reason. It does not matter, except that that question mark stands as the epitome of several controversies over the tale, especially its ending. Rabkin heads the few who have allowed for multiple possibilities for meaning; many critics since then have summarily dismissed not only the question mark, but also the possibility that "Jane" could have many meanings, assuming one or another.[4] A mysterious female identity becomes an irresolvable conundrum.

We will return to this very important and vexed question of "Jane" later. I have raised it early to suggest how "The Yellow Wall-Paper" lends itself to an analytical approach aligned philosophically with feminism but not yet directly employed in the published Gilman criticism: Derridean deconstruction.

Indeed, Gilman's story proves itself an ideal site for exploring three fundamental and interdependent tenets of deconstructive theory: that Western culture is phono/logocentric, privileging speech and presence over writing and absence; that *différance* results from attempts by utterances to capture ultimate meaning or "transcendental signifieds," creating endlessly deferred meanings, what Jacques Derrida calls "play"; and that this instability of meaning, in its futile attempts to solidify itself through language, only further disperses into *aporias* (undecidable textual cruxes). To demonstrate these dynamics, I will occasionally turn to the variants between Gilman's manuscript and the *New England Magazine* text to indicate how attempts by editors to rehabilitate impasses of meaning succeed only in creating more instability. A quick, though representative, instance of this would be the narrator's declaration that noticing a woman in the wallpaper gives her "something to expect," adding excitement to her tedious existence (MS, 339–40). When the magazine text adds a modifier, "something more to expect" (*NEM*, 356–57), a host of new but problematic cruxes arises: What "something" has *previously* been expected? The magazine also altered to "something else" (*NEM*, 375) Gilman's original phrase "another thing" (MS, 356) several lines later, when the narrator notices a strange smell emanating from her wall covering. Is this that same "something," earlier mentioned, or a different something? In Derridean terms, these efforts at making Gilman's usage consistent not only have not clarified meaning, they have removed it even farther away: there is *always* "another thing" standing between signifiers and their ultimate signification. In order to enter the text at an earlier unraveling point, then, I prefer to use Gilman's manuscript for interpretation.

+ + + +

Derrida insists that Western culture and language are both logocentric and phonocentric, cumulatively privileging presence of a speaker so that, for example, a conversation with a present friend is better than a telephone exchange with a removed one, which is superior to a letter from an absent one. Or, more tellingly, Yahweh's creation of the world by fiat ["word"] or his direct revelations to Moses have been followed by an increasingly corrupt transmission through burning bush, stone tablet, original scripture, translation, redaction, modernization, regularization, and modern dimestore editions. In considering the attraction deconstructive theory has for some feminists, one need look no further than Adam's direct reception of the covenant of works from God, and Eve's subsequent—and unchronicled, to boot—getting it second-hand from her husband. In short, women of the West have been encouraged neither to speak nor to listen in public, nor even to write. (Much fiction by female authors in the eighteenth and nineteenth centuries was produced pseudonymously. Nathaniel Hawthorne called them "a d——d mob of scribbling women" in his letter to publisher William Ticknor, in 1855.) Hence, while male-centered narratives tend to focus on the protagonist's search for a moral/ethical code or simply for identity, stories with female protagonists—who often seek expression as artists of some kind—can with some justice be collectively designated as a basic *search for voice*.[5]

John, the husband in Gilman's piece, clearly privileges presence over absence, speech over writing. In fact, he violates his Hippocratic oath—"do no harm"—by forbidding his wife to write. Of course, the presence he insists upon is the narrator's, not his own (she remains confined while he is often out on overnight cases), but the speech he favors *is* his own. His diagnosis of "a slight hysterical tendency" (MS, 16–17) typifies the discourse of dismissal he erects for his wife to inhabit as surely as she is forced to reside in their rented colonial mansion. John's adaptation of S. Weir Mitchell's rest cure could be construed as another manifestation of male incomprehension in face of a line of "sick," silenced women that stretches back at least as far as Aeschylus's *Agamemnon* (in which Cassandra's prophecies fall on deaf ears) and Sophocles' *Oedipus Rex* (when Jocasta departs the stage to hang herself, having futilely begged her husband to disregard *hearsay* evidence of his identity). The narrator's journal, or any kind of writing she might attempt to do, has no place here, as exemplified by the replacement of Gilman's original, crucial verb "write" in the sentence "So I will let it alone [thinking about her condition], and write about the house" (MS, 31) with "talk about the house" (NEM, 34).

+ + + +

Our narrator has been removed to a domicile in the country, ostensibly because extensive renovations to their permanent home have been undertaken for a three-month period (MS, 266). From the first sentence of her narrative, she finds impossible the task of pinning down the nature of this house for let, always aware that whichever word she chooses gains its effect of meaning only at the expense of (or through) the absence of other signifiers. Already we are reminded that Derrida's coinage *différance* is a portmanteau—meaning both "to differ" and "to defer." She first calls the house an "ancestral hall" (MS, 1) but immediately proceeds to a series of inadequate amendments: "A colonial mansion, a hereditary estate, I would say a haunted house" (MS, 3). None of these satisfies her descriptive sensibility, and for a while she relinquishes the effort to locate a final signifier, so that the house simply becomes "it." Even adjectives like "queer" (MS, 5) give way to two questions: the first concerns the price (an attempt to assign *value*)—"Else why should it be let so cheaply?"—and the second reminds us again that devaluation occurs without *presence*—"And why have stood so long untenanted?" (MS, 5–6). Notice that even the "it" has faded into a mere implied phrase by this, the fifth sentence of the story.[6]

The narrator's tentativeness is thematically appropriate here, of course, since Gilman relies on her imperfect perceptions to suggest that perhaps *none* of these descriptions is accurate, and the reader might interpret the nailed-down bed, "rings and things in the walls," barred windows, and other minor details as evidence that her bedroom is hardly a former nursery (or is it a gymnasium or playroom?) as she surmises, but a chamber with a more sinister history (MS, 65). But its most prominent feature is, of course, the wallpaper, which evokes descriptions so riddled with ambiguity that her previous attempts at real estate appraisal seem positively expert.

The paper's color, described only in the manuscript as "A sickly penetrating suggestive yellow" (MS, 353–54)—this sentence was conspicuously omitted from the magazine text—has connoted everything from urine to Chinese immigrants for various readers. Perhaps that very "suggestiveness" earned excision for the offending sentence, because it specifically invited readers to nail down something too disturbing, whatever it may have been, for a refined publication like the *New England Magazine*. "Old foul bad yellow things" (MS, 355) perhaps seemed more than enough to make the point.

Having noticed a pattern with a "certain lack of sequence, a defiance of law" (MS, 293–94), in the paper, the narrator muses, as she begins a new journal entry:

> If only that top pattern could be gotten off from the under one! I mean to try tearing it, little by little.
> I have found out another funny thing, but I shan't tell it this time! It does not do to trust people too much. (MS, 410–13)[7]

The last two passages quoted invite several observations. First, the pattern is not quite a pattern, is it? Without sequence or law, how can it be? Putting aside the question of what such a pattern may symbolize (some say patriarchy, others women's writing, still others the state of the narrator's mind), the wild configuration has somehow become two, one on top and one beneath. The adjective "certain" (which did not make the *NEM* cut) actually means "completely uncertain" to us, though it does indicate a kind of conspiratorial tone in context of the second paragraph, wherein the *other* "funny thing" is indefinitely deferred to another time, one which will never arrive, as we might intuit from the narrator's reaction to her discovery of Jennie considering the pattern: "I am determined that nobody shall find it out but myself!" (MS, 337). Finally, "gotten off" becomes immediately qualified as "tearing" in the manuscript (though not in *NEM*, in which she means only to "try it") and later as shaking (MS, 429), "pull[ing]" (MS, 431, 494), "peel[ing]" (MS, 432, 460), "finish[ing]" (MS, 435), "doing" (MS, 440), "touch[ing]" (MS 441), and "work[ing]" (MS, 451). Is it any wonder that such *différance* has rendered undecidable the narrator's motives and attitude toward the already-impossible-to-read pattern for the past century? We might also note, in passing, how the earlier "work," which has been forbidden by John and which most readers feel is self-evidently writing, seems to have been replaced by, or at least deferred to, this new set of signifiers, just as Derrida predicts.

In a neat bit of foreshadowing, Gilman has her narrator watch "the moonlight on that undulating wall-paper till it made me creepy" (MS, 255–56). The *New England Magazine*'s agents apparently did not make the connection to her many later declarations about the verb "creep," which, at one point, Gilman uses *seven* times in close proximity, clearly for repetitive effect (MS, 393–400). The magazine altered the present instance to "till I felt creepy" *(NEM*, 270), demoting the word to modify "fe[eling]," rather than to suggest a transformed "me." To *become* or *be made*—by mysterious wallpaper, no less—creepy—forces a consideration of just what "creepy" might be; but the magazine's copyeditors must have felt confident they knew, as they published their final illustration above the now-notorious alteration of the ending: "I had to creep over him *every time!*" (NEM, 532, emphasis added). In fact, the word is far more resonant than the synonym for crawling they took it for. The intent of such pre-interpretations by editors for readers is to resolve vagary into monolithic meaning, but in fact they only disperse meaning even further: What does "every time" mean, anyway? Until John awoke? Until others discovered the couple? Into perpetuity?

+ + + +

To return to my original point: We have now seen that "Jane" is only one among many of the aporias of the work known as "The Yellow Wall-Paper," but it is the most far-reaching in terms of interpretational consequences. My own interest in the manuscript text was, years ago, engendered by curiosity as to whether that was the name Gilman originally wrote. In fact, it was, as the text in this volume shows. In the remainder of this essay, after briefly discussing some traditionally perceived problems with deconstruction, I will attempt to show how "Jane"'s meaning in both the magazine and manuscript texts "unravels" each, respectively, and what that unraveling can accomplish for us. Of the many possibilities for "Jane," for the sake of space, let us provisionally throw out all but three. And let us stick, for the moment, to what might have made sense *to Gilman*. Those three possibilities are:

1. The proper name of Jennie, John's sister and housekeeper. Allan H. Pasco pointed out to me that the name derives from the same Hebrew root as John, meaning "the Lord's grace."
2. The narrator's own name. Until now, it has not been revealed in the story. This leads to at least two distinct lines of sub-possibilities:
   A. the narrator has been possessed by some kind of supernatural agent, probably the woman behind the wall-paper. This is the voice we hear reveling in its freedom: "I've got out at last[!]"
   B. the narrator has become schizophrenic, referring to herself in the third person.
3. The name of the baby.

The first two, suggested by Rabkin in the 1960s and much elaborated by later critics, will be supplemented by the third: I have deliberately chosen something that pushes the responsible interpretive envelope in order to emphasize how deconstruction, to borrow a more useful comment from the great romancer Hawthorne, does not confine itself to the *probable* in human existence, but, so long as it does not violate the "truth of the human heart," has what is *possible* for its scope.[8] And there are undoubtedly many more meanings that have not occurred to me and would probably not (or could not) have occurred to Gilman. In true deconstructive fashion, a group of students once informed me that the events of the story do not actually occur at all, except in the drug-induced, paranoiac delirium of the narrator. When I suggested that the phosphates John has prescribed for her would probably not have hallucinogenic side-effects, they countered by asserting the narrator smokes marijuana. Their evidence? Combine the single mention of "Mary" early in the tale with the single, cryptic reference to "Jane" at its conclusion—what other explanation could there be?! My mentioning in class the similarities to the Edgar Allan Poe tale "Ligeia," in which the narrator regularly imbibes opium, had unwittingly suggested the reading!

Deconstructive theory has been perceived as problematic because it raises the specter of *relativism*. By relativism, I mean the philosophical concept that there is no absolute truth; and even if there were, human beings are too subjective, too affected by their own biases and the limitations on their senses, to share that truth. In one of literature's famous lines, Hamlet declares "there is nothing either good or bad, but thinking makes it so." Similarly, Satan of Milton's *Paradise Lost,* upon being cast into Hell: "The mind is its own place, and in itself can make a heav'n of hell, or a hell of heav'n."[9] The way relativism plays out in classrooms is that students, and often very bright ones, become silent: they begin to feel as if their opinions don't matter, because everyone has one, and everyone has a right to one. Who are they to pretend to know what the work means? Or, in place of silence, interpretations based on *impression* replace those based on *evidence.* The unrecognized irony in both cases is that these students go on to take courses with professors operating on the formalist assumption that some opinions are better than others, that some evidence is more compelling toward certain conclusions, that there is a truth worth investigating. My own (admittedly subjective) experience tells me that dedication to relativism is a necessary phase through which many intelligent people pass, primarily instilling tolerance in them, on their way toward finding their personal value system. But, if this stopping place in our journey is extended too long (as in Odysseus's rest in the land of the lotus-eaters), paralysis begins to set in: we become comfortable with the idea that arguments are not worth making, and our readings of texts and situations become lazy and facile; worse, we may move to the position that ethics and morals are arbitrary, and actions no longer worth performing.

If deconstruction raises the hackles of professional readers and teachers, it has not done well historically either, or at the opposite end of the political spectrum from the "anarchism" outlined above. In the 1980s its detractors even tried to tie it to Nazism following the death and discovery of letters by Paul de Man, a spokesman for the theory who turned out posthumously to have possible ties to the fascists in World War II Belgium. Without becoming mired in old arguments, it is possible to test the value of deconstruction on individual texts by using it in the way it works best: to track backward, through one work, the consequences of an important aporia on several established readings and one new one.

In its own time, and through much of the twentieth century, "The Yellow Wall-Paper" was read by many as a tale of gothic horror. However, I share with many post-1973 feminist critics[10] the assumption that the story equally concerns itself with sexual politics: that is, the struggle for power between the narrator and her husband over her rights in marriage. These two readings[11] are, of course, not mutually exclusive: what could be more horrifying than confinement in a life without rights? But we have often acted, perhaps for the purpose of combating relativism, as if only one reading is correct. In any event, this particular marital power struggle has probably been going on for years previous to the narrative's opening, but is brought to a head by the birth of the couple's child and their subsequent removal to a country house to treat her "temporary nervous depression,—a slight hysterical tendency" (MS, 16–17), a condition modern readers often recognize to be misdiagnosed postpartum depression.

Dr. (the husband is an M.D.) John's diagnosis is followed by the prescription for complete rest: "I take phosphates or phosphites—whichever it is, and tonics, and journeys, and air, and exercise, and am absolutely forbidden to 'work' until I am well again" (MS, 19–21). By "work" she means writing, as we find out a few lines later, as she informs us she has continued to do it secretly (MS, 26–27). But readers of the magazine text and its descendants have had to puzzle out the recognition that this is epistolary fiction, that she is writing *now*, in a journal that we, the audience, are studying: the magazine changed "I will write about the house" to "I will talk about the house" (MS, 31; *NEM*, 34). Note the potential confusion generated by choices in language: the alteration by the magazine may have made the tale more Poesque, the prattling voice of a deranged mind calling out to us from the depths of madness. Surely the addition of ninety new paragraph breaks, which makes the beginning of the story, especially, graphically more fragmented than the manuscript, added to this effect. But the substitution of "talk" for "write" also tends to downplay the major question of the power struggle, the narrator's *right to write*, to communicate her feelings, to express herself, to retain autonomous value in her life aside from duties as a wife and mother. Of course, what rights does a madwoman have? Again the magazine amplified this suggestion by adding the words "every time" to the story's ending for the purely decorative effect of making its columns end flush (see fig. 4).[12] John has found the key and gained entrance to his wife's attic bedroom, in which she has locked herself and torn down the disturbing wallpaper, and fainted at her declaration that she has freed herself. John swoons, "and right across my path by the wall, so that I had to creep over him!" (MS, 497–98). Gilman might have hoped to suggest at least two possibilities: that the narrator would crawl over her husband on the way out the door to her (at least temporary) freedom; or that she would remain in the room with him until he returned to consciousness, undoubtedly to face more stringent confinement and a downgraded diagnosis from "hysteria" to "insanity." The magazine virtually shut down the first possibility by adding "every time" after "creep over him," in keeping with its attempts to monolithize meaning (except for the mistake with the question mark)—in this case the meaning that the narrator is, or becomes through the course of the tale, insane.

Having juggled a bare summary of these two fairly standard readings (feminist and gothic), let me elaborate what I think the multiple possibilities for "Jane" add to our understanding.

(1) "Jane" as the proper name for Jennie. Any good gothic needs a villain. A gothic is a form of Romance, and (to oversimplify a bit), modern romantic fiction—which shares some conventions with medieval romances—is set in a universe ruled by competing forces of God and his adversaries, of good and evil. The country estate, which the narrator has been tempted to call "a haunted house, and reach the height of romantic felicity" early in the account (MS, 3–4), is a staple of the genre, the location wherein the struggle between the chaste heroine and the paternal villain is played out on his own ground. The house is traditionally a woman's refuge, her sphere, and this displacement and enforced unfamiliarity shakes her own foundations, evoking irrational fears that nothing she has previously taken for granted is as it seems, including the goodwill of men and the sisterhood of women. The gothic villain, maniacal though he may be, is a creature of the mind, of the rational, often of science. He does not deign to sully his hands and so often employs a henchman to serve him (in this case his sister, a servile representation of himself). The employment of a hench(wo)man is of course the manifestation of his own psychological imbalances, of his denial of his own physicality and therefore sexuality (which in considering perverse he succeeds in perverting). The magazine would crystallize this impression by altering Gilman's manuscript version of John picking the narrator up and carrying her "in his strong arms" up to bed (MS, 228). The magazine merely reads "in his arms" (NEM, 241), just as at the manuscript's conclusion, when John cries for an ax to "break that beautiful strong door" which separates him from his wife (MS, 482), the magazine deletes "strong" for the second time, as if to deemphasize John's own physical potential (NEM, 518). In short, John is the head and Jennie the "hand," or body. Jennie performs the functions of housekeeper, whose duties include washing the yellow stains from the clothes, and whom the narrator catches "with her hand on it once" (MS, 328).

When one reads the story alternatively as a feminist allegory, in which the patterns of the wallpaper confine the woman behind, suggesting the patriarchal oppression of all women, the declaration that allies "Jane"/Jennie with John ("I've got out at last, in spite of you and Jane!") raises an important point *about* patriarchy. According to M. H. Abrams, patriarchy (rule by the father) defines society as

> male-centered and controlled, and . . . organized and conducted in such a way as
> to subordinate women to men in all cultural domains, religious, familial, political,

economic, social, legal, and artistic. The female tends to be defined by negative reference to the male as the human norm, hence as a kind of non-man, by her lack of
the identifying male organ, of male powers, and of the male character traits that
are presumed to have achieved the most important inventions and works of civi-
lization. . . . Women themselves are said, in the process of their being socialized, to
internalize the reigning patriarchal ideology (that is, the set of conscious and unconscious presuppositions about male superiority), and so are conditioned to dero-
gate their own sex and to cooperate in their own subordination.[13]

Early in the story, the narrator laments that John's diagnosis that "there is really
nothing the matter" is confirmed by her own brother, "also a physician and also
of high standing" (MS, 15–18). This collaborative endorsement of the status quo
by men is brought beyond a simplistic "men vs. women" dynamic by the introduction of Jennie as complicit agent of patriarchal values. She remains "a perfect—,
an enthusiastic—, housekeeper, and hopes for no better profession" (MS, 154–55).[14]
Having internalized the traditional options and beliefs about her proper place,
Jennie stands as a foil to the narrator, eventually acting as a kind of guard or jailer.
In time, she is removed from the estate and the story with the other tools—"So
now she is gone, and the servants, and the things" (MS, 446)—after having served
her purpose, only a bit less subordinate than "servants" and "things" (except in
magazine-based texts, where all are equated by added syntax; see NEM line 476).

(2) If "Jane" refers to the narrator herself, these readings are not substantially
altered. (A) The story as Gothic would have had precedents for spiritual possession: again, Poe's "Ligeia" is such a story, in which the ghost of the narrator's first
wife returns to inhabit the freshly deceased body of his second. In "The Yellow
Wall-Paper," the narrator has observed a woman within the wallpaper: one night,
as John sleeps, "[t]he faint figure behind seemed to shake the pattern, just as if she
wanted to get out" (MS, 257–58). What enables the narrator to see the figure is
moonlight, which "creeps" through all the bedroom windows as the moon travels
through the night sky. The manuscript has the narrator "watch[ing] the moonlight
on that undulating wall-paper till it *made me* creepy" (MS, 255–56, emphasis added),
a significant grammatical construction when one considers how essential the *act*
of creeping is in the story: first the moonlight creeps, then the mysterious woman,
and finally the narrator herself. However, the magazine's editors altered the reading to "till I *felt* creepy" (NEM, 270; my emphasis), muting not only the foreshadowing effect of the original but also the suggestion that the narrator is herself
undergoing some kind of transformation (or transmigration).

(B) The feminist allegory can accommodate a complicity in the narrator's
own oppression (what Marxist critics call "self-colonization") in addition to that
previously attributed to John's sister, Jennie. "John" and "Jane," two of the most

common names available, could easily represent not only two people within a marriage but the respective genders of men and women themselves, within the marriage institution. Some feminists have suggested that the woman behind the wallpaper is a projection of the narrator's feelings of resentment and helplessness, a sort of psychological doppelgänger. A passage about halfway into the story clearly demonstrates the mental degeneration that accompanies this identification between doubles: "I think that woman gets out in the day time! And I'll tell you why —privately—I've seen her! . . . I see her on that long road under the trees, creeping along, and when a carriage comes she hides under the blackberry vines. I don't blame her a bit. It must be very unpleasant to be caught creeping by daylight! I always lock the door when I creep by daylight" (MS, 391–400). The psychic distance between the two women will progressively diminish until the story's climax, but at this relatively early point the magazine made another unaccountable change, substituting the word "humiliating" (NEM, 424) for the original "unpleasant." To my mind, the manuscript reading indicates a narrator who, while she may be imagining this woman whom she observes through her windows, still cannot identify completely with her, choosing the relatively inarticulate "unpleasant" to imagine the woman's fear of being caught. The magazine, however, tends to prematurely collapse that distance by specifying the more empathetic "humiliating." In NEM's case, the eventually freed woman can justifiably declare to John that she has gotten out "*at last*, in spite of you and Jane!" (my emphasis) because Jane, that is, that part of the narrator which represents women in general, has refused, despite an acute sense of its suffering, until quite late in the day to help free the part of herself that suffers from day-to-day oppression.

(3) The final possibility I would like to propose for "Jane" is that it applies to the other unnamed character in the story: the narrator's baby, from whom she has been (voluntarily?) separated. Now, many readers may at this point sign off from my argument, citing the seemingly indisputable pronoun evidence, which does not differ between the manuscript and magazine texts: "It is fortunate Mary is so good with the baby. Such a dear baby! And yet I can <u>not</u> be with him, it makes me so nervous" (MS, 95–97). Two things about this passage are remarkable. First is the sole mention of Mary in the work. Who this is, whether a wetnurse, another sister of John's or the narrator's, the holy mother (a cryptic suggestion that the baby, who is *never* present, has died and passed into her hands), or an early mention of the sister that was overlooked and never regularized during revision, is impossible to say.

Second and more interesting is that Gilman goes out of her way never to identify the baby's gender again, as in the following passage: "There's <u>one</u> comfort, the baby is well and happy, and does not have to occupy this nursery with the horrid wall-paper. If I had not used it that blessed child would have! What a fortunate escape! Why, I wouldn't have a child of mine, an impressionable little thing, live in such a room for worlds. I never thought of it before, but it is lucky that John kept me here after all. I can stand it so much easier than a baby you see!" (MS, 234–41). Given all the narrator's other supposed delusions—her belief that she is confined in a nursery, for example—I do not consider it much of an interpretive leap to propose that she may have confused the gender of the "impressionable little thing" in her sole pronoun reference (as is often done with pets). Or, that she may have said "him" as a psychological projection of what she wanted but did not receive, a male child who would grow up in a male-centric world with more autonomy than his own mother; this would also account for the resentful tone of "in spite of you and Jane!" *Or,* remarking the lack of pronouns elsewhere, we can return to the original reference and note that "him" could actually refer only *to John* (who has been the main subject of the contextual discussion) and that the baby's gender is *never* identified. The magazine's mangling of Gilman's paragraphing does not help matters here. The manuscript reads:

> It does weigh on me so not to do my duty in any way. I meant to be such a help to John, such a real rest and comfort, and here I am a comparative burden already! Nobody would believe what an effort it is just to do what little I am able. To dress and entertain and order things. It is fortunate Mary is so good with the baby. Such a dear baby!
>
> And yet I can <u>not</u> be with him, it makes me so nervous.
>
> I suppose John was never nervous in his life. He laughs at me so about this wallpaper! At first he meant to re-paper the room, but afterwards he said that I was letting it get the better of me, and that nothing was worse for a nervous patient than to give way to such fancies. (MS, 91–101)

Not to be overly ingenuitive, but "him" is exactly, verbally equidistant between "baby" and "John": eight words from each. And clearly John is often referred to as either "he" or "him," while the baby never is except possibly in this sole instance. Grammatically, one tends to assign a pronoun to the last person named ("dear baby"), but we see time and again in this story how the narrator's thoughts often run according to associative patterns and counter to established logical and grammatical patterns. It seems just as likely to me that, as she reflects on how she has failed to help John according to the dictates of her social "duty" as a doctor's wife, the narrator utters a stray thought about the baby, but returns to rationalize her failure as wife (*not* as mother) as a result of her nervous condition. She cannot "be with" John as he attends to his social duties.

I recognize, of course, that I have been on purely speculative ground for some time now as I follow this interpretive line. But this story, much like a poem, has more "gaps" than most (lapses in information that the reader must supply), as evidenced by my very topic: Who is Jane? This raises a crucial point about deconstructive reading, which, like almost any tool, can be used in a wrong way and in a right way. The wrong way is to destroy a text, to argue that it is meaningless. The right way is to "unravel" it, to argue that it has crucial contradictions, ambiguities, and undecidabilities that undermine the authority of any single interpretation or claim to truth about it. Far from nullifying the close readings of the past, deconstruction invites us to read even more closely and discover new possibilities. In doing so, deconstructors do not bind themselves to readings that seem (subjectively) "likely" or "convincing" or that need to accord with an author's possible intentions. Deconstructive readings can be anachronistic, ahistorical, and even absurd on the surface (which accounts for the puns and humorous contemporary references often employed, a side-effect of the "play" of language), as long as they rely on textual evidence. The point of this is not to ridicule works, their authors, or the professional critics who read them but to open up their possibilities for meaning by, as the popular phrase goes, thinking outside "the box" (I will leave the many possibilities for *this* little aporia to the reader's imagination).

The proof of deconstruction's usefulness is in what "Jane" as the baby *does for* the story. In her sixth journal entry, about two-thirds of the way into the work, the narrator evokes a good deal of sensory imagery. First, she remarks the various shades of color of the fungi in the wallpaper, in the sentence that was deleted from the magazine printing: "A sickly penetrating suggestive yellow" (MS, 353–54). She continues: "It makes me think of all the yellow things I ever saw—not beautiful ones like buttercups, but old foul bad yellow things" (354–55). One can only speculate as to why the magazine's agents dropped the sentence, but especially the words "penetrating" and "suggestive" could connote, among other things, a hint of sexuality. Next, the narrator immediately ruminates on the smell of the paper: "very gentle, but quite the subtlest, most enduring odor I ever met" (MS, 364–65). And it is here that the allusion to Brontë's *Jane Eyre*, and its madwoman in the attic, Bertha Mason, appears: "I thought seriously of burning the house to reach the smell" (MS, 367–68). Is this the smell of some ghostly ectomorph, of complicit patriarchy, or of something more corporeal and visceral? The smell gets into the narrator's hair. Finally, the tactile sense is invoked by the yellow smooch that runs around the room low on the wall, and which at the climax the narrator will have fitted herself into. "Round and round and round—round and round and round," she confusedly notes, "it makes me dizzy!" (MS, 374–75). All this sensory data seems random observation—until, that is, one considers that her final emergence/escape from the wallpaper can be construed as a kind of psychic, if not physical, *(re)birth*: "I've got out at last, in spite of you and Jane!" Here the gothic and the feminist readings undergo a convergence. The narrator, in the persona of the woman trapped behind the four walls of the domicile or "nursery," attempts time and again to break through to a selfhood unrestricted by patriarchy. But the birth canal is blocked, not only by the domesticated self that already stands without, but by the infant whose care defines the most important role of that self. And all three are born into a world where girls are, in a real sense, monstrosities: creatures of emotion, fancy, and irrationality, who must be held in check by their patriarchal wardens. Only after baby Jane's delivery can the voice of the Afterbirth—"another thing" in its guise as monstrous feminine, who offends the senses even as she awakens the newborn to them—be heard, acting as her own midwife. Whatever happens to baby Jane, she will grow up between a mother either absent or too crippled to care for her, and resented by her gorgon "sister" simply for existing.

The theme I take away from the story is supported, not undermined, by the multiplicity of interpretations of "Jane." It concerns fragmentation—that splintering which accompanies the denial of one's identity by oneself or others. "Jane" is offered as the ultimate failure to mean. The very undecidability of Jane's identity *is* the point, in a society that denies woman the basic right to construct her own self, but instead defines her by a host of successive and partial labels: child, wife, housekeeper, mother, nervous hysteric, madwoman, monster. The work, by demanding interrogation and refusing to tie itself up with single, convenient answers, invites not only its own deconstruction, but that of its variant texts, its author, her culture, and our own.

Notes

1. *NEM* lines 529–30, corrected to "Jane!" in this edition. Parenthetical references to Gilman's manuscript (MS), "The Yellow Wall-Paper," Charlotte Perkins Gilman Papers, Schlesinger Library, Radcliffe College, Cambridge, Massachusetts, and the *New England Magazine* 5 (January 1892): 647–56 (*NEM*), refer to line numbers of the critical texts printed in this edition. I have argued elsewhere, in "Gilman's Manuscript of 'The Yellow Wall-Paper': Toward a Critical Edition," *Studies in Bibliography* 51 (1998): 259–73, that Gilman never read proofs for the magazine printing, and so all variants between her manuscript and *NEM* are assumed in this essay to be changes made not by the author but exclusively by the magazine's agents.

2. In American literature, one need look no further than Thomas Jefferson and the Declaration of Independence to see how variant texts further complicate already-complex passages. What does "all men are created equal" mean? Concentrating only on "all"—citizens? of the white

race? who owned sufficient property?—presented a conundrum for readers as proximate as the framers of the U.S. Constitution. Jefferson's *Autobiography* (published 1829) reveals that the draft of the Declaration included in its charges against King George the foisting of the "execrable commerce" of race slavery on the American colonies. The passage was removed from the draft at the insistence of South Carolina's delegates to the Continental Congress, who refused to sign until it had been stricken. In short, the already aporic "all men" meant one thing when Jefferson penned it and quite another when it was "engrossed in parchment" just a few days later.

3. Leslie Y. Rabkin, ed., *Psychopathology and Literature* (San Francisco: Chandler Publishing Company, 1966), 111.

4. However, when the problem is not avoided entirely, increasingly more complex interpretations have emphasized multiplicity, which indicates just how loose a thread the name is. Conrad Shumaker, "'Too Terribly Good to be Printed': Charlotte Gilman's 'The Yellow Wallpaper,' *American Literature* 57 (December 1985): 588–99, identifies Jane as "the wife she once was" (597). William Veeder, "Who Is Jane? The Intricate Feminism of Charlotte Perkins Gilman," *Arizona Quarterly* 44 (Autumn 1988): 41–79, was first to diagnose schizophrenia: "[Jane] is both her own sister-in-law Jennie and the woman in the wallpaper" (65). Jeannette King and Pam Morris, "On Not Reading between the Lines: Models of Reading in 'The Yellow Wallpaper,'" *Studies in Short Fiction* 26 (Winter 1989): 23–32, refer to the exclamation at the conclusion as "this first and only use of her name, here expressing the conflict between the heroine's two selves" (28–29). Margaret V. Delashmit, "The Patriarchy and Women: A Study of Charlotte Perkins Gilman's 'The Yellow Wallpaper'" (Ph.D. diss., University of Tennessee, 1990; *Dissertation Abstracts International* 51 (12): 4120A), acknowledges the major interpretations and merges them: "If John's wife is named Jane, then the fact that his sister is named Jennie is further indication that doubling is intended since the name Jennie is the diminutive form of the name Jane. Also, if the narrator's name is Jane, then her schizophrenic character is even more easily ascertained as she abandons her Jane self to assume a nameless identity" (200).

5. "Jane" bursting out at the end is a dramatic manifestation of presence (and will force the reader to recognize at this point, if she has not already done so, that the final journal entry is not written at all, but rather narrated with a sense of immediacy the story has heretofore lacked). See also Denise D. Knight's discussion of Chopin's *The Awakening* and Freeman's "The Revolt of 'Mother,'" in this volume, for the female search for voice.

6. Later, the narrator will make more attempts at a transcendental signified for her temporary home. Apparently impatient waiting for her to do so, *NEM*'s agents attempted to clarify her pronoun "it" (MS, 49) by making it "the place" (*NEM*, 53).

7. Incidentally, the passage shows again the narrator's preferred phrase for the wallpaper's many phenomena—"another (funny) thing"—this time overlooked for regularization by *NEM*'s compositors.

8. Nathaniel Hawthorne, *The Centenary Edition of the Works of Nathaniel Hawthorne*, vol. 2, preface to *The House of the Seven Gables*, edited by Fredson Bowers, Matthew J. Bruccoli, and L. Neal Smith (Columbus: Ohio State University Press, 1965), 1.

9. John Milton, *Paradise Lost*, in *The Works of John Milton*, vol. 2, pt. 1, edited by Frank Allen Patterson (New York: Columbia University Press, 1931), I.254–55. William Shakespeare, *Hamlet*, in *The Globe Illustrated Shakespeare* (New York: Greenhouse House, 1983), 2:2.

10. The year 1973 marks the publication of the Feminist Press edition, containing the text that inaugurated the flood of modern criticism, beginning with Elaine Hedges's afterword.

11. This is not to imply that the work has been interpreted exclusively in one of these two ways. Scholars and teachers have found many inventive contexts. For example, Mary C. Carruth, "Teaching the Politics of Difference and 'The Yellow Wall-Paper' in Women's Literature Courses," in *Approaches to Teaching Gilman's "The Yellow Wall-Paper" and* Herland, ed. Denise D. Knight and Cynthia J. Davis (New York: MLA, 2003): 143–51, relates both the gothic genre and Gilman to the American slave narrative tradition, represented by Harriet Jacobs's *Incidents in the Life of a Slave Girl* (146ff.).

12. See St. Jean, "Gilman's Manuscript," 267n15, for a fuller explanation of how typographical concerns alone can cause textual variants.

13. M. H. Abrams, *A Glossary of Literary Terms* (Fort Worth, TX: Harcourt, Brace, 1993), 208.

14. See Denise D. Knight's essay, also in this volume, for an analysis of the variant forms of this phrase (p. 77).

Contributors

Catherine J. Golden is a professor of English at Skidmore College, where she teaches Victorian British and American literature. She is the author of *Images of the Woman Reader in Victorian British and American Fiction* (2003) as well as the editor of five books, including, most recently, *Charlotte Perkins Gilman's* The Yellow Wall-Paper: *A Sourcebook and Critical Edition* (2004). She is currently launching a book on Victorian postal culture.

Denise D. Knight is a professor of English at SUNY Cortland, where she teaches nineteenth-century American literature. She is the author of *Charlotte Perkins Gilman: A Study of the Short Fiction* (1997) as well as the editor of a two-volume edition of Gilman's diaries (1994). Knight has been the recipient of numerous awards, including SUNY Chancellor's awards for Excellence in Teaching and Excellence in Scholarship.

Allan H. Pasco, the Hall Professor of Nineteenth-Century Literature at the University of Kansas, is interested in prose fiction of the eighteenth through the twentieth centuries, although his research extends to other forms of literature, to cultural studies, and to critical theory. His most recent book, *Sick Heroes: French Society and Literature in the Romantic Age, 1750–1850* (1997), traces Romanticism to dysfunctional families, and his current project focuses on eighteenth-century attitudes toward love. He has published half a dozen books and many articles in such journals as *PMLA, New Literary History, Comparative Literature,* and the *Virginia Quarterly Review.*

Shawn St. Jean is the author of *Pagan Dreiser: Songs from American Mythology* (2001) and has published articles in *Feminist Studies, James Joyce Quarterly,* and *Studies in Bibliography,* among other journals. His next project will track various modes of social criticism employed by American authors and filmmakers. He has worked as a cook, a carpenter, a soldier, a mechanic, and more recently, a teacher for the past twelve years and is now an independent scholar.

Index